SUPERNATURAL LORE
OF OHIO

STEVEN J. ROLFES

THE
History
PRESS

Published by The History Press
Charleston, SC
www.historypress.com

First published 2020

Manufactured in the United States

ISBN 9781467144148

Library of Congress Control Number: 2020938674

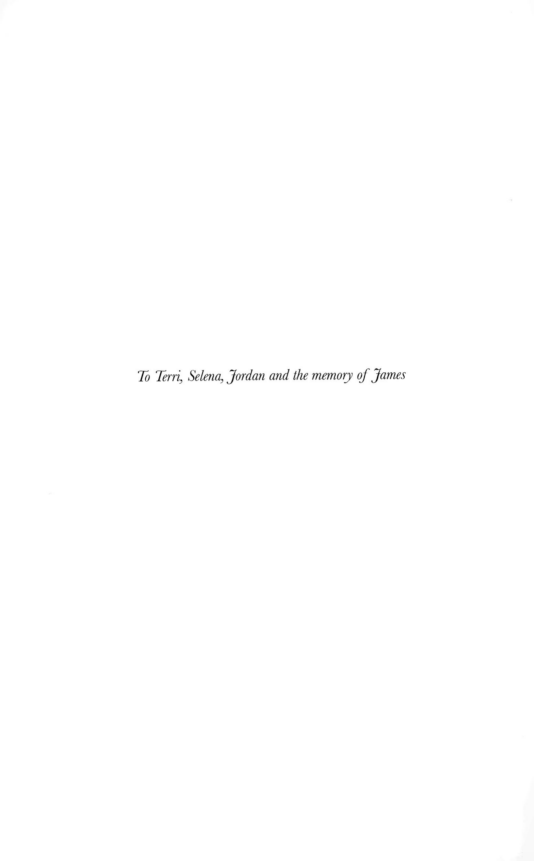

To Terri, Selena, Jordan and the memory of James

CONTENTS

ACKNOWLEDGEMENTS

I would like to thank my very patient editor, John Rodrigue, as well as Hayley Behal and Diane Mallstrom and all of the great people at the Public Library of Cincinnati and Hamilton County, Jordan Rolfes of Beagle Rampant Productions for his photography, technical and editing support, Selena Rolfes for her photography and Terri Rolfes for her technical support. A very special-thank you to Douglas R. Weise for driving me all over Ohio to take pictures of strange and weird places and Ron Hill of the Clermont County Historical Society and Sandra DeVise with the Cincinnati History Library and Archives of the Cincinnati Historical Society for her assistance with the research on *A Sermon on Witchcraft*. I also thank the good Lord for keeping all things in the natural and supernatural realms in harmony.

THE GREAT SERPENT MOUND

Which when the Lord God heard, without delay
To Judgement he proceeded on th' accus'd
Serpent though brute, unable to transferre [sic]
The Guilt on him who made him instrument
Of mischief, and polluted from the end
Of his Creation
—*John Milton,* Paradise Lost

Leaving the wagon, we scrambled up the steep hillside, and pushing on through
bush and briar were soon following the folds of the great serpent along the
hilltop. The most singular sensation of awe and admiration overwhelmed me at
this sudden realization of my long-cherished desire, for here before me was the
mysterious work of an unknown people, whose seemingly most sacred place we
had invaded.[1]
—*F.W. Putnam*

Welcome to the strangest place in Ohio.
The world is full of ancient sites of forgotten spiritual power—sacred places where the natural and the supernatural overlap. Some may be surprised to know that one of the most mysterious enigmas left to us from ancient people is located in Adams County in central Ohio—that perplexing earthen monument known as the Great Serpent Mound.

To add to the mystery, this location is apparently not random. Sometime in the late Carboniferous or early Permian epochs, about 300 million years ago, a meteor slammed into the earth at the exact spot that would later house the monument.[2]

Seeing the mound from the ground is rather unimpressive, as it only rises to 3 feet. However, after climbing the observation tower and seeing it from above, one discerns the figure of a gigantic snake that is 1,348 feet long. The tail is coiled into a spiral, much like the designs seen on some megalithic stones in Great Britain. The other end, the head, is a massive triangle, apparently representing the serpent opening its mouth to swallow something. This intended feast is an egg-shaped earthwork located just outside of the snake's mouth.[3]

Among those who have wondered at the meaning of this megalith was Frederic Ward Putnam, the curator of Harvard's Peabody Museum of Archaeology and Ethnology. Looking to the religious symbolism of the serpent, he wrote, "Was this a symbol of the old serpent faith, here on the western continent, which from the earliest time in the religions of the East held so many people enthralled, and formed so important a factor in the development of succeeding religions?"[4]

To compound the mystery, Putnam noted that the Great Serpent Mound is not entirely unique. There is another similar prehistoric earthwork of a long serpent, but it is rather doubtful that there was ever any contact between the other builders, as the other snake is located in Argyllshire, Scotland.

While the two groups of ancient people did not communicate with each other across an ocean, there is little doubt that their versions of the same monument served a practical and spiritual function. Both serpents' heads point west, and the tails end in the same baffling spiral. Following the greatest mass of the body would allow one to calculate the time of the various solstices. The head of the serpent marks the sunset at the summer solstice, while the end of the spiraling tail marks the rising of the sun at the winter solstice.[5]

Aside from being a calendar, it has been hypothesized that the monument also serves as a compass. The shape of the snake has been connected with the constellation Draco. The bright star in this group, Alpha Draconis, more commonly Thuban, was employed in ancient times as the North Star.

While it was undoubtedly a temple, a calendar and possibly a compass, one thing that the great serpent was *not* was a burial place. There are countless Indian burial mounds located throughout Ohio, but excavation work at the site has not revealed any burials.

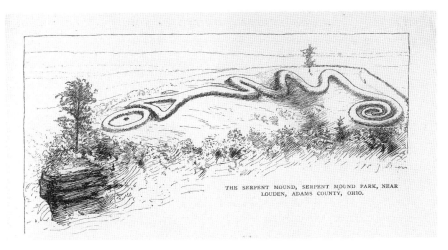

THE SERPENT MOUND, SERPENT MOUND PARK, NEAR
LOUDEN, ADAMS COUNTY, OHIO.

A sketch of the Great Serpent Mound in Adams County. *From the collection of the Public Library of Cincinnati and Hamilton County.*

The mysteries are endless. Even the most basic question remains unanswered: who built this mysterious effigy mound? This fundamental issue is a source of contentious debate. As there are no skeletons or artifacts to guide investigators, the matter must be answered by other means. Some archaeologists have evidence to prove that the architects were from the Adena culture (800 BC–AD 100). Other scientists have equally strong proof that the builders were from the more recent Fort Ancient culture (AD 1000–1650). If one visits the mound on a day when there are two groups of scientists working at the same time, beware—at any moment, they might start throwing rocks at each other, defending their particular theories.

The bigger question remains unanswered: why was this monument constructed? Why a serpent?

Theories of the purpose abound. Reverend Edmund Landon West was convinced that this spot in central Ohio was the actual location of the Garden of Eden. In 1909, the preacher stated that there was no doubt that this was a representation of the Genesis serpent in the Garden of Eden, which was located at this exact spot. The oval shape by the mouth, he postulated, was the forbidden fruit. To back up this unique interpretation, he turned to scripture: "By his spirit he hath garnished the heavens; his hand hath formed the crooked serpent."[6]

The good reverend seemed to have forgotten that Eve ate the fruit and then gave it to Adam, who, in Eve's defense, was right next to her and did absolutely nothing to stop her. There is no mention of the serpent eating the fruit.

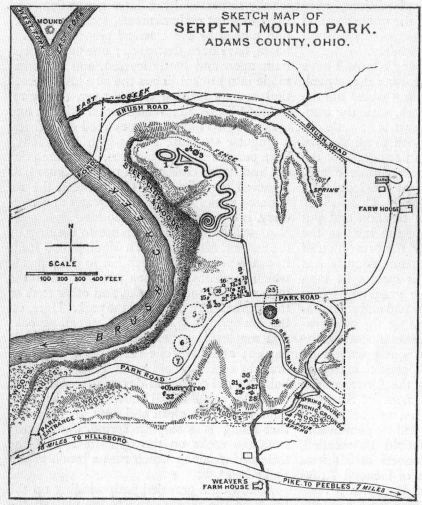

1, The Oval Embankment in front of the serpent's mouth. In this inclosure is a small mound of stones. 2, The Serpent. 3, A low Artificial Mound near the head of the serpent. 4, A very small Artificial Mound just west of 3. 5, 6, 7, Ancient Excavations, appearing like sink-holes. 8, 19, 20, 21, 22, 23, 24, and in space bordered by 18, 15, 20, 21, are Sites of Ancient Habitations. 9, Burnt Stones on the clay. 10, A recent Indian Grave over two graves. 11, Portions of Three Skeletons in a pile. 12, 13, Skeletons in the clay. 14, Grave with Two Skeletons. 15, Grave with Skeleton, over which was an ash bed. 16, Pieces of a large Clay Pot. 17, Small Burial Mound. 18, Several small Excavations in the clay, filled with dark earth. 19, 24, See above. This Village Site was afterwards found to extend 200 feet east and south. 25, Burnt space under the dark soil extending to the edge of large conical mound. 26, The Conical Mound, a monument over a single body. 27, 28, Cremation Places in the clay under the dark soil. 29, 30, 31, Very Ancient Graves deep in the clay. 32, Small Mound over four ancient graves in the clay.

Putnam's map of the Great Serpent Mound and the surrounding area. *From the collection of the Public Library of Cincinnati and Hamilton County.*

Visitors have come from all over the world to gaze at this mystery from the past. Preserving the monument has been a struggle over the years. Putnam and other early archaeologists fought to have the State of Ohio guard the integrity of the mound. In 2008, the United States submitted the Great Serpent Mound and some other Native American earthworks to be included in UNESCO's prestigious World Heritage List. Ohio's baffling serpent would join such marvels as the Giza Pyramids, Stonehenge, the Taj Mahal and the Great Wall of China.[7]

The protection of the mound is certainly necessary. Some people do strange things at ancient spiritual sites. In 2012, a New Age group called Unite the Collective buried a number of "muffin-crystal-thingies" in the mound. Yes, that is what they actually called them. These were small muffin-shaped devices that were intended to "reactivate" the "orgone" or spiritual energy of the great serpent.[8]

The philosophy behind this relates to the teachings of modern mystic Wilhelm Reich. Reich preached that *orgone* was a life force similar to the concept of chi or prana. Reich sold devices to enable people to use their orgone. This quickly attracted the attention of the U.S. Food and Drug Administration, which, in the 1950s, prosecuted Reich as a modern snake oil salesman.[9]

Visitors today are not allowed to go beyond a barrier and actually walk on the mound, but sadly, members of the orgone-activating collective blatantly disregarded these rules. At the same time that they were burying their devices, other members of the group were hopping up and down on the fragile monument as though they were children at a playground. Not only did this cause damage to the ancient site that people were trying so hard to preserve, but it also showed extreme disrespect to the Native Americans who labored to build the effigy and regarded it as a spiritual center of their existence.

The group was so proud of its actions that it posted a video of the event on YouTube. However, it has since been taken down, possibly because someone realized that they were providing evidence of a crime.

In 1987, at the time of the Harmonic Convergence, numerous New Age devotees visited the serpent. These people were well behaved and respectful of the site. They preferred meditation to trespassing.

Like many megalithic monuments, the Great Serpent Mound has more than its share of supernatural events. Just walking along the visitors' walkway around the great serpent, one might feel somehow out of place, as though intruding on a space where people have no business.

In 2014, a young man and his girlfriend snuck into the area after dark. Having heard about numerous supernatural occurrences in the monument, including UFO sightings, they wanted to see it for themselves. They were not disappointed. At first, they heard a buzzing sound, which became louder as they approached the mound. (They did not disrespect the people who built the mound by crossing the barrier.) Soon, they saw three balls of orange light following the shape of the serpent, going from head to tail over and over again. As this was happening, both could detect a curious burning smell in the air.

When the girlfriend inadvertently made a noise, one of the balls of light suddenly stopped. In an instant, all three of the lights shot up into the air, and just as quickly, they were gone.[10]

Art Caruso from Youngstown, accompanied by three female assistants, was granted permission to take scientific measurements of the serpent. They must have picked the wrong day, as a series of bizarre events took place. One assistant, a young woman named Sue, actually vanished in front of Caruso. She reappeared a moment later, stating that Caruso had disappeared to her. Another assistant, Beth, went into a trance and began to converse in a strange language.

These phenomena are reminiscent of the events that occurred to Paul Devereux and his Dragon Project team doing work at various prehistoric megaliths in Britain, particularly at the Rollright Stones at the Oxfordshire-Warwickshire border. Among the inexplicable events experienced at this megalithic site was the sighting of a ghost gypsy caravan.[11]

There have been many other supernatural experiences reported over the years. Many people who visit the serpent have glimpsed curious shadows moving about. Some have heard the footsteps of those people who labored to build the monument. Even walking along the pathway around the serpent, some sensitive people claim to feel a kind of energy emanating from the ground.[12]

Whatever the original purpose of the Great Serpent, there is no doubt that this is indeed one of the most mysterious sites in the world—and certainly one that is worth a visit.

Thus in this mystifying and apparently haunted spot near Chillicothe, we begin our journey to the strange side of the Buckeye State. Let us now proceed to a banquet of the bizarre—the supernatural lore of Ohio.

1
A SUPERNATURAL BUFFET

VAMPIRES, BANSHEES
AND THEIR KITH AND KIN

And there shall the beasts of the desert meet with the jackals,
and the wild goat shall cry to his fellow; the Lilith also shall settle there,
and find for herself a place of rest.
—Isaiah 34:14

Today popular culture, films and books portray the vampire as a teenage heartthrob—an alluring, sexual creature with Mephistophelean charm. However, when looking at actual cases of vampirism in the Old World, there is nothing romantic or seductive about the entity. The overwhelming consensus is that the undead creature does not bring about lovesickness—it causes death and decay.

The vampire is a parasite, a demonic being trapped in a limbo state between life and proper death and an entity that steals the vitality from its victim to sustain its own unnatural existence.

According to folk belief, witches, as well as those who committed suicide and those who led lives of incredible evil and ungodliness are sometimes doomed to return after their deaths, hungry and desperate to steal the life from the living to prolong their own depraved being. This revenant is quite different from what we see on movie screens today.[13]

There are only a very few cases of vampirism in the United States. But there are *some*, and before proceeding with Ohio's undead, we should pause to take a quick trip to New England to look at two of the United States' most famous vampires.

The district most noted for this phenomenon in this country is the gloomy, heavily forested region of Rhode Island known locally as the Nooseneck Country. It is from this tiny area of the smallest state in the Union that we find two American vampires.

Certainly, the most bizarre is the 1799 case of the Tillinghast family. The father, Stukeley, was a prosperous farmer in the Rhode Island town of Exeter, located deep in the Nooseneck Country. One night, he suffered a dreadful nightmare in which he dreamed that half of the trees in his orchard withered away and died right before him.

Real life followed this dark prophecy—not concerning trees but rather his children. The first one to waste away was his nineteen-year-old daughter, Sarah. Some say the cause was tuberculosis while others believe that something even darker was responsible for her demise.

Sarah had always been a bit different; the young lady was a loner and a bit on the dreamy side. Her favorite activity was to wander about alone in the local Revolutionary War graveyards and sit on gravestones while reading sad poetry. In fact, she had done this on the very day that she first became ill. Nothing could save the poor girl, who soon died from a wasting disease. She was buried by her grieving family—but that was not the end of it. Indeed, it was only the beginning.

Soon, her younger brothers and sisters were all telling a tale of horror. They each swore that their dead sister Sarah was coming to their beds in the night and sitting on their chests. The first one to complain of this was little James, but soon his siblings all said the same thing.

One by one, they wasted away, and one by one, they followed Sarah to the cemetery.

Finally, it was decided that no matter how horrible the idea was, the bodies of Sarah and the others must be exhumed and examined for signs of vampirism, as prescribed in folk belief. All of the brothers and sisters were decomposing normally. But when they came to Sarah, they were in for a shock. She had been dead for eighteen months, yet the corpse had not decomposed at all. It looked as though she had just died or was simply sleeping in the box. Stukeley and his farmhand Caleb then cut her chest open and removed her heart. It was filled with liquid blood.

The heart was burned, and the poor girl was reburied. However, by now Stuckely's terrible prophecy had come true—he had lost exactly half of his orchard. Six of his children now lay in the cemetery. There were no further cases in the household.[14]

A century later, in the same area of Rhode Island, there was another account of vampirism—the most famous of all. Mercy Lena Brown, often referred to by her middle name, was a nineteen-year-old girl living in the small town of Exeter. Members of her family began to waste away and die. As with the Tillinghast incident, some today state that it was consumption (pulmonary tuberculosis) that affected the family. Others whispered that it was a case of vampirism.

Mercy, who, like Sarah, was only nineteen years old, died on a Sunday morning in January 1892. Unlike Sarah, she was not the first in her family to perish; her mother and older sister had already wasted away to death. Her brother had started to show symptoms and attempted to escape by fleeing to the clean air of the mountains of Colorado.

Once again, the rumors of vampirism began to circulate through the Nooseneck Country. Permission was requested to legally exhume the bodies. This macabre appeal was dutifully granted, and on St. Patrick's Day 1892, the bodies of the recently deceased Browns were removed and inspected. All had decayed normally—except for Mercy.

Thinking that they had found the vampire, the family had her heart removed and then burned on a nearby boulder. Some of the ashes were mixed into a broth and fed to her ill brother, who had returned from the West. Despite this unconventional medical treatment, he died two months later.[15]

Mercy's grave in the Chestnut Hill Baptist Church cemetery has become something of a tourist spot, with visitors leaving various gifts and flowers for America's most famous vampire. Her gravestone is now secured to the ground with an iron band after vandals tried to steal it. The Tillinghast family plot is not as easy to locate, as it is in what is known simply as Historical Cemetery Number 14. The names on the sandstone markers are almost completely worn away, making it impossible to identify which one is Sarah's.

Whether Mercy Lena Brown was really a vampire or a poor girl who died of pulmonary tuberculosis is a matter of debate. While she may not have lived forever as an undead bloodsucker, she has achieved immortality through the writing of one of the United States' greatest authors of the supernatural, H.P. Lovecraft. Mercy was obviously the inspiration for his famous short story "The Shunned House." Indeed, Lovecraft even used the first name Mercy for one of his characters—in this case, as the head of the cursed house.

The prominent Cincinnati abolitionist Reverend Moncure Conway wrote at length on the subject of demonology. In his seminal two-volume work *Demonology and Devil Lore*, he chronicled a suspected case of vampirism in Chicago:

> *Dr. Dyer, an eminent physician of Chicago, Illinois, told me (1875) that a case occurred in that city within his personal knowledge, where the body of a woman who had died of consumption was taken out of the grave and the lungs burned, under a belief that she was drawing after her into the grave some of her surviving relatives. In 1874, according to the* Providence Journal, *in the village of Peacedale, Rhode Island, U.S., Mr. William Rose dug up the body of his own daughter, and burned her heart, under the belief that she was wasting away the lives of other members of his family.*[16]

However, the bizarre occurrences in Rhode Island may not have been as remote as one would like. Few people remember that there was a similar case in Ohio's Scioto County.

This 1816 case involved a young Swiss immigrant named Samuel Salladay, son of Philip Salladay. Both of these men died from the wasting disease of consumption. After their deaths, the corpse of Samuel was disinterred by Major Amos Wheeler of nearby Wheelersburg. The body was then cut open, and the entrails were pulled out. These were burned, and the ashes were eaten by the surviving members of the family. This event was thus described:

> *The Salladay family were afflicted with consumption, and had a family burying ground on a ridge, at the lower line of the old farm. Samuel Salladay had died during the fall of 1815 and was buried there. Two or three months after they took him up and took out his heart, liver and lungs; they were burned up in fire prepared for the purpose, the family sitting round while they were burning, hoping it would arrest the disease. Mrs. Curran* [a woman of the Salladay family who had married Matthew Curran and lived on a portion of the Salladay property] *was not present, but she and her sister, Mrs. Bradshaw, died within a year. George Salladay was the only one that lived to a reasonable old age.*[17]

The famed historian Henry Howe, a New Englander who moved to Cincinnati in 1848, also described this gruesome scene:

This was accordingly done in the winter of 1816–17, in the presence of a large concourse of spectators who lived in the surrounding neighborhood, and by Major Amos Wheeler, of Wheelersburg. Samuel Salladay was the one they disinterred and offered up as a sacrifice, to stop if possible the further spread of the disease. But like other superstitious notions with regard to curing diseases it proved of no avail. The other members of the family continued to die off until the last one was gone except George.[18]

What prompted the alarm of vampirism in this case is a matter of conjecture. In neither surviving account is there any mention of the dead people returning to the living members of the family. But there must have been something to drive people to disturb the peace of the grave and perform such gruesome acts on their deceased loved ones.

These dreadful events are a far cry from the vampire depicted today in popular media, where the entity is invariably presented as a glamorous and often sophisticated person, thought to be a desirable mate (except for the inconvenient fact that the person is both dead and a lethal parasite). We must leave the world of *Twilight* behind and take a look at a peculiar haunted house case from northwestern Ohio.

In examining this case, one must bear in mind the creature described in folk belief. More properly defined by the Greek *vrykolakas*—literally "wolf fairy"—the vampire is a spiritual being, sometimes manifesting in the form of a resurrected corpse, and at other times remaining as a spirit that steals the life from its victim. In 1885, it was reported that there was a house in which everything was inexplicably wasting away, including the residents.[19]

The tiny village of Van Wort is built over an area known as the Black Swamp. One might conjecture that the pestilent nature of the landscape brings to mind hungry spirits desiring to feed off of the living.

The house in question was not some gothic castle or forlorn manor but rather a simple log cabin. However, unlike the other similar structures in this swampy area, this one seemed to be haunted—and whatever was haunting this cabin was hungry.

A farmer named Goodloe came to this area with his family, leaving behind Pottsville, Pennsylvania. It is not certain if he built the cabin himself or purchased it ready-made from someone else who had decided on a quick change of address. What is certain is that almost immediately, he and his wife and children all began to "lose flesh," a rather poetic description of literally wasting away. After approximately three years of trying to make a living in this land at the house, the entire family resembled skeletons.

Goodloe's wife had been urging him to leave their cabin and return to the safety of Pennsylvania. Finally, he relented and left the cursed house. He did not abandon Ohio but built a new house far away from the old one, still on the same land. The idea worked, and after that there was no further trouble with his family.

He then rented the old cabin to an elderly African American farmer, who was delighted to win such a good bargain. However, this was a definite case of buyer beware. The new tenant hit the road in half a year, saying that the house was haunted.

While the people may have been ill from natural causes of disease, this does not begin to explain the other manifestations of the haunted cabin of Van Wort. Not only were the people wasting away, but everything else that had any semblance of life was doing the same. The hogs, although well fed, were becoming progressively thinner. They were finally set out into the countryside to feed, and their old home was boarded up to prevent them from returning to the cursed abode.

Finally, the hogs gained enough weight that they were butchered, and the meat was hung up on joists in a smokehouse. However, whatever was stealing life from the human occupants also had a taste for ham. The meat was found to be shriveled up and wasted away.

It would seem that nothing that was alive could stand up to this attack. It was not only humans and animals who suffered from the predations, but plants as well. Fruit trees planted near the house withered away, twisting about to resemble mere sticks protruding from the ground.

As Goodloe stated after he left the cabin: "I could notice a difference in my corn crop this fall. I had a pretty fair yield all around, excepting the part of the field which was near the cabin. Close to the cabin the ears were nothing more than nubbins, and mighty poor ones at that. I'll bet I shingled that old house more than half a dozen times in the three years that I lived in it. Every time the shingles would warp and draw out the nails and finally drop off."[20]

Perhaps the weirdest part of this account is that when food was placed on the stove, it would shrivel up and curl until there was seemingly nothing left. With the warping shingles, people, pigs and even plants wasting away, it is safe to assume that this was no mere case of tuberculosis.

In January 1897, there was yet another case of victims mysteriously withering away in Ohio. This was in Lucas County on Lake Erie. In a small village known as Richfield Center, seventeen families, mostly of German origin, suffered from the same wasting disease. To make matters even more perplexing, just as in the Van Wort occurrence, some of their animals were also deteriorating. The residents believed that this illness was the result of an evil spirit, what would be known in their folk beliefs as an *alp*.

Then the demon apparently showed itself. A physical manifestation of this attack was the mysterious presence of a black cat. Unnaturally large, it was seen prowling around infected homes. One family tried to escape the curse by moving to the barn to sleep, but they were chased back into the house by the vicious feline.

One resident, A.M. Miller, was transported by carriage to Toledo, looking for medical help. He was literally wasting away and was so weak that he could barely walk. If the old beliefs could not stop the attacks, then perhaps modern science could.

He was examined by physicians, some of whom journeyed to Richfield Center and examined the other people in the village. After all, how often does a medical doctor have the opportunity to battle a vampire? After thorough examinations, they could find no rational cause for the wasting away of both humans and animals; however, they were still certain that it was a natural disease and not vampires or witchcraft.

There is a significant addendum to this occurrence. The people who were afflicted began to take their feather beds outside of their homes and burn them. As we will see in a later chapter, this is an obvious reference to the curse of the feather crowns and the fear of sorcery.[21]

It is hard to say what one should think of the supposed encounter between a man and a vampire that purportedly occurred east of Dayton near the town of Yellow Springs, Ohio, in 1879. The account of the meeting seems to be a tall tale, but it was dutifully reported in the newspaper as an actual event.

A man named William Wilkson was riding home at night when his way was blocked by a mysterious figure in black. The creature, seeming to be a man, had a long beard and especially long and threatening nails. Both the nails and other parts of him were covered in blood.

Wilkson entered in a struggle with him, including attempting to stab him with a bowie knife, all to no avail. Finally, he spoke to the creature, demanding to know what it wanted with him.

At once, the creature stopped fighting and confessed his sinful existence. He was a vampire by his own admission and proceeded to tell Wilkson a fantastic story of once being a mortal man four thousand years earlier. At this time, he broke the biblical law and drank blood. He began by first drinking the blood of animals that he killed and then he eventually moved on to humans. He first murdered his child and drank the blood, followed by his wife.

The self-professed vampire lived in that manner for a few years, craving more blood. Finally, he was captured by the authorities, tried and put to death—although the means of this execution are not given.

From here, he described his passage into the existence as the undead:

> *I awoke to another state of being—but that terrible craving still remained! I became conscious of the fact, and then I knew what it was to be in hell! O, the agony I suffered! Think not that I was beyond my power to do further evil—that I was debarred from sin. I tell you that I had the same power of slaughtering my fellows, of being the same vampire at their mangled throats! O, how my demoniacal capabilities were increased! How rapidly I progressed in the downward change from man to beast! I could see, by the reflection of my features, that they were becoming the features of a beast of prey!*[22]

He claimed that an angel appeared to him and released him from his bondage of bloodlust. After saying all of this, he simply vanished, allowing Mr. Wilkson to continue his journey with a wild story to tell.

Suicide was often closely related not only with restless ghosts but also with vampirism. In January 1892, a Cincinnati man named Geise went to the German Protestant Cemetery (now known as the Walnut Hills Cemetery, located on the corner of Victory Parkway and Gilbert Avenue, not far from Xavier University). Possibly to save the authorities the trouble of transporting his body, he stood over a grave and committed suicide.

However, his soul was unable to rest. For some time after that, his ghost was seen floating about over the grave where he had killed himself. Word spread about the apparition, and soon, people dared to enter the haunted cemetery in the dark of the night to catch a glimpse of the specter. Many were not disappointed, as they clearly saw the shade of the man still lingering over the place where he had taken his own life as though he was somehow unable to move away from that terrible spot.[23]

While the apparition in the Walnut Hills Cemetery did not interact with the living, a far more frightening and baffling specter appeared in Cincinnati in 1889. This occurred in what is now known as the Gaslight District of Clifton. Whether this wraith was a witch, a ghost or an evil spirit in human female form is up for debate. Whatever it was, it had powers that were definitely not human.

The victims in this case were two teenage brothers who lived near Resor Avenue. The pair always walked home on a certain path near a field owned by Captain Robert Hosea. However, one day they found a mysterious woman standing there, blocking their way. She was dressed entirely in mourning black, and her face was covered with an extremely thick material so that none of her features was visible. The only bit of color on her was a single white feather in her hat.

The brothers looked at each other and then decided to continue their journey. However, as the boys timidly approached the apparition, she suddenly motioned for them to stop and go no further. They halted and decided to turn around and return home by a more indirect route.

After some days of using the alternate route, the two decided that they would go the old way and see if the wraith was still there. They went at different times, and the first boy arrived home safely and waited for his brother. His brother, however, did not arrive.

Gathering as many people as he could, the first boy went back to the pathway to search. They found his brother lying unconscious on the ground. He was carried home and nursed back to consciousness.

In a frightened voice, he told the people that he did not see the mysterious lady in black. However, as he walked through the area that she had warned them to stay away from, he was suddenly struck by a powerful unseen force that knocked him to the ground. The next thing he knew, he was home, lying in his bed with his family and all of these people looking down at him.

A few days later, the two rather stubborn boys once again ventured into that forbidden area. The first indication that something was not right came from the side of the pathway. A stump that was known to produce phosphorus light from decaying material was suddenly glowing and was brightly visible even though it was daylight. As soon as this started, the two boys looked ahead and once again saw the strange apparition, which had not been there before. What was worse, she was now moving steadily toward them as if angry. They turned tail and ran, vowing to forever find a different way home.[24]

One of the unusual supernatural creatures reported in Ohio is known as the Werewolf of Defiance, a city in the northwestern corner of the state. In July 1972, two railroad men were working in the yard one night when a creature, part human but mostly wolf, attacked them. Curiously, although the monster had good-size claws and fangs, he used a club. After the initial encounter, he ran off swiftly and vanished into some brush.

Not long afterward, another railroad man saw the lupine creature lurking in the yard. A week later, a man saw the beast in his headlights.

The police did not find much humor in the matter and searched for the creature. Naturally, officers dismissed it as a man in a mask, although the reports of fangs made that rather unlikely. They thought that a local person might be involved, but as they were the police, they should have been familiar with any person who would do such a thing. Their investigation failed to turn up a local person or a transient.

After that, as most of these flaps go, the creature just vanished. There were no further reports.[25]

Certainly, one of the creepiest denizens of the otherworld is the *bean sídhe*, or the banshee. An import from Celtic lands, particularly Ireland and Scotland, this is the female wraith who will wail before a person dies. Sometimes she is seen washing blood out of the clothing of a person doomed to die.[26]

One legendary account of a banshee is the one who predicted the death of the great Irish hero Cuchulain: "They came to a ford, and there they saw a young girl thin and white-skinned and having yellow hair, washing and ever washing, and wringing out clothing that was stained crimson red, and she crying and keening all the time. 'Little Hound,' said Cathbad, 'Do you see what it is that young girl is doing? It is your red clothes she is washing, and crying as she washes, because she knows you are going to your death against Maev'e's great army.'"[27]

The most famous instance of a banshee appearing in the Buckeye State occurred at the Old Courthouse in Dayton on North Main Street. The building is known to be quite haunted. People have heard ghostly moaning there and have even heard the footsteps of those who were making their final walks to the gallows. The rear of the 1850 building is said to be haunted by the restless spirit of John McAfee, who had the dubious honor of being the first man to be hanged in public in Montgomery County.[28]

One of the most inexplicable Dayton executions was that of a young murderer named James Murphy in August 1876. The night before the Irishman was to be hanged, the peace of the jail was shattered when a banshee wailed for him. The deafening scream was heard not only by the other prisoners but also by Deputy Sheriff Hellriggle, who was on duty in the block. The other prisoners were not at all happy with the midnight concert, and it took quite a while to restore calm in the jail.

The next day, Murphy was taken to the gallows and hanged—twice. The first attempt, although seemingly impossible, resulted in the rope breaking. Another rope was brought out as quickly as possible. The condemned man was picked up from the ground, led back up the thirteen steps and hanged a second time.

This time it worked.[29]

This is not the only banshee case in Ohio. Closely related to the Celtic bean *sidhe* is a supernatural creature called a fetch, a variation of the Scandinavian entity known as a *fylgja*. This is an evil spirit in animal form that will go around to fetch the soul from a dying person. As it turns out, one of these may have been prowling the hallways of the City Hospital in Cincinnati.

In 1892, a Mr. Gailor wandered into the hospital complaining that he had recently heard the screaming of a banshee. He wanted to look over the facility to see how he might be a patient in the near future. After he looked around, he left, never to be seen by them again. The employees just shook their heads and muttered about how the crazies were out today.[30]

Was he crazy? Perhaps something came looking for him at the hospital and decided to stick around. The same people who had laughed realized that they had another visitor—one who would soon become unwelcome and very frightening.

The Old Courthouse in Dayton. Numerous executions occurred here, resulting in not only hauntings but also witnesses clearly hearing the wail of a banshee. *Library of Congress.*

This unexpected visitor was an ink-black cat. It just appeared in the hospital one day after Mr. Gailor's visit and would not leave. At first, the workers adopted it as a kind of mascot, feeding it and allowing it to roam freely about the hallways.

However, soon the staff was not as happy with the feline caller. The night clerk, Hudson, was connected to the various wards with a telegraph. Whenever a patient died, he would be notified with a special signal on the device. One night, the black cat began to make a terrible ruckus in the basement. Hudson went down to investigate. As soon as he returned to his desk, the telegraph went off announcing the death of a patient.

This was hardly remarkable, but it continued to happen. Every so often, the normally calm feline would unexpectedly let out screeches and howls for no apparent reason. As soon as it did, the clerk would invariably receive a telegraph stating that a patient somewhere in the hospital had left this world.

The black cat was no longer as popular as he once was. The gloomy feline was soon given a name: Death.[31]

Among the supernatural creatures roaming the byways of Ohio, perhaps the most famous and most bizarre is the entity popularly known as the Loveland Frog or sometimes Frogman.

There had been scattered, unverified reports of an uncanny reptilian humanoid near the Little Miami River in Loveland for many years. No one took them too seriously until February 1972, when police officer Ray Shockey was on patrol near the river and saw the creature. It scurried away and disappeared into the predawn darkness. A week later, another officer, Mark Matthews, saw the same creature. He thought it was a dead animal in the roadway. When he tried to investigate, the thing sprang up and scurried over a guardrail into the river. A local farmer also saw the form during this same time period.

It was described as less than four feet tall and a bipedal. Some said it was similar to the Hollywood creation *Creature from the Black Lagoon.*

The two officers changed the story slightly over the years, no doubt after growing tired of being asked about it. Matthews later claimed that he had shot it, and it was definitely an iguana.

Some have speculated that it was a hoax, while others have hypothesized that it was an iguana. This is quite unlikely, especially as these sightings were in February. Whatever it was, it has certainly become part of Ohio folklore. One can purchase T-shirts stating that they have seen the Frogman. There is even a Frogman marathon.[32]

Château Laroche, popularly known as the Loveland Castle, was built in modern times by World War I veteran Harry D. Andrews. *Photo by Douglas R. Weise.*

While in Loveland searching for oversized humanoid reptiles, one might want to visit another peculiar site, the Loveland Castle. This medieval-style castle located right on the Little Miami River (where the Frogman supposedly emerged from) does have a few haunts connected to it, even though it is a modern construction. The chapel has a curious flowery smell to it, and there have been reports of hauntings, albeit somewhat playful.

A group of Cub Scouts spent the night in the facility. When they woke up the next morning, they found that something had tied all of their shoelaces together in the night.

The castle is properly known as Château Laroche, after a medical facility in France during World War I. A veteran of that conflict, Harry D. Andrews, built his castle over a number of years. It was willed to his Boy Scout troop, known as the Knights of the Golden Trail.

It was Harry Andrews himself who experienced some of the first hauntings. Some visitors to the castle have seen a shadowy thing with glowing eyes outside of the structure watching from the woods by the river.[33]

In the tiny city of North College Hill, there was an encounter with one of the strangest and rarest supernatural entities, the doppelgänger. This is a

27

double of a living person, and to see it is usually an omen of an imminent death. The Japanese call this entity the *ikiryō*, a ghost of a person who is still alive but soon will not be.

The Cary sisters, Alice and Phoebe, lived on the Clovernook farm before growing up to both become celebrated poets. One day, the family was coming in from the fields when they saw two family members standing in the doorway waiting for them. When they arrived, they found that neither person was in the doorway. Both of the people died months later.

The Cary Cottage has been preserved as a historical site. Witnesses have seen a girl in an old-fashioned dress looking out of the window of the house.[34]

There have been other reports of doppelgängers in Ohio. In 1977, a young woman saw her mother come home at eleven o'clock at night. Later, her mother came home at dawn, apologizing for being out all night. A young woman in Marion saw her sister with her hair in a towel and wearing a robe come from the bathroom toward her bedroom. When she later went to borrow a record from her, she found no trace of her sister, nor was there a towel or robe. When she asked her mother, she was told that her sister had been at work all day.[35] Thankfully, no deaths resulted from this baffling encounter.

No supernatural entity could be as memorable as a good old-fashioned headless horseman. Turns out, one does not have to journey all the way to upstate New York to see the headless horseman—Ohio's roadways are haunted by more than one of these specters.

Cary Cottage, the childhood home of poets Alice and Phoebe Cary. This was the site of an appearance of a doppelgänger. *Photo by Jordan Rolfes.*

Like the banshee, the tradition of the headless horseman goes back to ancient Irish beliefs. Human sacrifices were made to the dark chthonian god Crom Cruach. The victims were decapitated or had their heads smashed with a stone, and then their blood was spread around the fields to bring fertility in the next year.

The sacrifices were performed on the Killycluggin Stone until the sixth century, when St. Patrick smashed it. The actual stone is now on display in the Cavan County Museum.

However, Crom Cruach was not put completely out of business by the appearance of the good saint. He became a creature known as the *far dorocha* ("dark man") or simply the Dullahan. He rides on a headless horse at night, and is himself without a head. He holds a jack-o'-lantern to light his way.

The Dullahan, similar to the banshee, would ride up to the house of a person destined to die. He would whisper the person's name by the window, or sometimes the locked doors of the house would open for him. He would enter the dwelling, speak the name of the person he was to take and then leave. When this happened, the person whose name was spoken had no hope—death was coming very soon.[36]

American writer Washington Irving visited the British Isles in the early nineteenth century. Inspired by these grisly tales, he decided that America needed its own Dullahan. He set his story in the Tarry Town area of New York in that gloomy woodland known as Sleepy Hollow. His tale, "The Legend of Sleepy Hollow," became one of the first classic American ghost tales. Generations of children have shuddered to hear Irving's description of the tormented spirit of a Hessian horseman whose head was taken off by a cannonball: "Gigantic in height, and muffled in a cloak, Ichabod was horror-struck on perceiving that he was headless! But his horror was still more increased on observing that the head, which should have rested on his shoulders, was carried before him on the pommel of his saddle!"

One of these horsemen is said to haunt State Route 38 in Yatesville. The area is sometimes referred to as Cherry Hill due to the number of cherry trees in an adjoining orchard, but more often, especially among the local teenagers, it is called Ghost Hill.

The story states that this was the ghost of a federal law enforcement agent who was murdered in the line of duty. He was investigating a counterfeiting operation run by members of the Funk family. His head was cut off, and the body was dumped into a well. One of several women who witnessed the murder received an axe to the chest to keep her from talking.

The inn where the murder occurred was shunned as haunted. People would claim that they saw ghosts walk into the building, and some even said that they peeped through the windows to see the specters sitting at a poker game.

Since that day, the headless ghost of the murdered government man has been seen riding madly up and down what is now State Route 38 and the backways of the area. An old farmer in the area, William Selsor, claimed to have seen the headless horseman many times over the years. Other residents agreed.[37]

There are two somewhat similar headless horseman stories from two different counties, although the distance between the two is not great. One tale may have borrowed from the other.

In Guernsey County, we find the city of Freeport near U.S. 22. This roadway is said to be haunted by a headless horseman. This began soon after a horse was found running down the road with no rider to be seen. When the horse was stopped, it was obvious that the saddlebag, which had earlier contained gold, had been cut. Obviously, there had been foul play somewhere on the road.

The area has been haunted by the headless horseman ever since. However, unlike the demonic Hessian who terrifies Ichabod Crane, this one may be good. Whoever sees him will dream of the gold that was stolen. Unfortunately, the alarm clock will invariably go off at exactly the wrong moment. No one ever dreams of where exactly the loot is hidden.[38]

A bit to the north at Woods School, near the city of Belmont, there is yet another gold-searching headless horseman. He is apparently one of three or four men who sold horses and, flush with gold, were headed to Belmont for a night on the town.

They didn't make it.

All of them disappeared, obviously having fallen prey to robbers who knew about the sale and the cash being carried by the men. Since then, the roadway has been haunted by a headless horseman—but not nearly as obliging as the one near Freeport. This one makes the traveler stop and demands to know where his gold is.[39] The remains of some cut-open saddlebags were found near Woods School in the 1920s.

The best known of all of Ohio's headless horsemen is the one nicknamed Stumpy, who haunts a region that has since become known as Stumpy's Hollow, near Norwich. The area is a small ravine just behind a Presbyterian church. It is thought that this ghost is the spirit of Christopher Baldwin, a librarian who had the dubious honor of being Ohio's very first road fatality after he died in a carriage accident on August 20, 1835.

Baldwin, a representative of the Antiquarian Society of Massachusetts, was headed to Zanesville to make a study of some of the Indian mounds in the area. However, a group of hogs being driven to market frightened the horses of the stagecoach, causing it to topple over. Perhaps the residents of the mounds did not want their rest to be disturbed.

Stumpy has made his presence known numerous times over the decades since his death in the early 1800s. One country doctor was so frightened that he leaped out of his carriage when Stumpy suddenly appeared in the seat next to him.[40]

While Ohio has a number of headless horsemen, it also has a headless horse without a rider. One can find this unsettling specter in the Rogues Hollow area of Wayne County. As the story goes, the horse was having a jolly time galloping down the road when it failed to notice the low-hanging branch of a tree. The poor animal was decapitated but continues its romp at night.

Sometimes the devil himself is seen riding the headless horse—a fitting steed for the prince of darkness.

Micky Walsh, whose father ran a popular tavern in the area, was herding a team of mules down the haunted roadway. Suddenly, the mules stopped and refused to go any farther. Walsh did his best to coax them to move, but they would not budge.

Then he saw what the problem was—the devil was sitting on the overhanging branch, looking down at him. Not wishing to debate the point with his infernal majesty, Walsh managed to turn the mules around without too much trouble and quickly left the area.

He told his friends of his supernatural encounter. They all had a good laugh, thinking that he had consumed a bit too much of his father's wares, but when challenged, they all agreed to take a ride down that dark road to see what diabolic phenomena they could witness. They proceeded, not expecting to find anything. However, they did indeed see something. It was, as Micky said, the devil himself. He was not in a branch but sitting on top of the famed headless horse.

Sometime later, the tree blew down and was completely blocking the roadway. By now, everyone in the Rogues Hollow area knew about the story of the devil sitting on one of its branches. No one was brave enough to try to move the tree or even touch it. The very next day, the haunted tree was gone. It had completely vanished as though it had never been there.[41]

This is certainly not the only personal appearance of the devil in Ohio. One of his most famous encounters occurred in McArthur in 1886 at a revival at the Macedonia church. The dark lord was described in traditional manner—gigantic with a dark black color and long horns.

He simply appeared in the church and refused to leave until prayer was offered for him.[42]

In the 1800s, there was something horrible lurking around the furnace at what is now the Lake Vesuvius Recreation Area in Lawrence County. While some reports state that it was a monster, others stated that it was none other than the devil himself. He blocked the road to keep the miners from their work. This happened for a few days in a row, interrupting the business of the mine. The owners took matters into their own hands and summoned a priest.

The good father confronted the diabolic entity. Rather than cowering in fear or running away, the father demanded to know what he wanted and why he was bothering honest people trying to go about their business. The two had a short conversation, and the devil left, but no one recorded what the demon said.[43]

European folklore has numerous tales of miners whose work was thwarted by underground spirits known as kobolds. Many times, mining activity was halted by interference from those supernatural entities that dwell in the darkness beneath the earth and sometimes do not like intruders into their realm.

Thus we have met the devil in Ohio. Now, let us look at a few of his employees.

THE SCALES OF INJUSTICE

*One may see occasionally even in Cincinnati a horseshoe nailed over a doorway
to prevent invasions from the spirits of the air. On some quiet street he may be
amused to see an old German woman, after pouring a bucket of foul water into
the gutter, stop at the door of her house and carve in the air with a knife. The
woman is convinced that by this process she succeeds in driving off those evil
beings that carry sickness wherever they go.*[44]
—Cincinnati Gazette, *1879*

People had come in from the farms of the surrounding countryside, one
wagon after another. Women were gathered in small groups gossiping
while keeping an eye on their small children who were running in the grass,
yelling and roughhousing. Men were in small circles as well, sharing and
commenting on the news of the day, the weather and the crops. Other people
stood close to the action, wishing to have the best view when the proceedings
began. After all, this was something that they could tell their grandchildren
about. How often does one see a real witch?

To top it off, the day might end with a hanging.

Thus began the very first time a person in Ohio was put on trial for
witchcraft. The year was 1805, and the place was Bethel, a small village in
rural Clermont County. If the stories were true, then apparently the devil
had found his way to the Buckeye State.

Modern people who look back on the events of that day can't help but
chuckle, noting a close connection between reality and a famous scene in

Monty Python and the Holy Grail. In the beloved film, a woman was tried for witchcraft by weighing her against a duck. In Bethel, the same method, substituting a Bible for a duck, was used to determine whether an elderly woman was a witch.

While some today may laugh, a serious observer will find nothing to grin about in these proceedings. Far too many elements of this case resembled the witchcraft trials of Salem and the resulting bloodbath. It was only through good fortune and sense, to say nothing of a belief in both the power of God and the rule of law—including the law of physics—that this tragedy was not repeated in Ohio.

In 1805, the village of Bethel, named after the sacred place where Jacob had the vision of the heavenly ladder and Abram built an altar to the Lord, had only existed for seven years. The community was founded by Obediah Denham. Obediah was a deeply religious man who had left Kentucky in disgust over the vile institution of slavery. He made sure not only that there would be no hint of slavery in his settlement but also that land would be set aside for worshiping God.

But even in Obediah's Eden the serpent slithered in.

Nancy Evans was an elderly woman living alone in a small cabin at what is now the intersection of Routes 125 and 232. She was a normal lady of her time, tending a small garden and caring for the one loyal friend in life—her cat. Unfortunately, her cat was black.

The problem came not from her, as she and her feline companion were simply minding their own business, but rather from her next-door neighbors, the Hildebrands. Just as in the tragic case in Salem 113 years earlier, the Hildebrand family included some young girls. It was their wild accusations that helped to bring about the potentially deadly legal proceedings.

The problems began with a woman named Jenna Beck, who had a quarrel with Helga Hildebrand. It was believed by some that Helga had hexed Jenna's heifer, causing it to die. Throughout history, witches have often been accused of killing livestock and destroying crops.

After this, Jenna became ill with strange fits and accused Helga Hildebrand of being a witch. A visit from a minister put a temporary stop to Beck's attacks, which included shouting blasphemies. However, the soothing influence of the clergyman ended with his departure, after which the attacks returned. This happened twice, with people now starting to look at the Hildebrand clan with suspicion.

At this point, seemingly to distract attention from herself, Helga started to have hysterical fits. Claiming that she, too, was the victim of witchcraft,

The small, peaceful town of Bethel narrowly missed becoming Ohio's Salem. *From the collection of the Public Library of Cincinnati and Hamilton County.*

she pointed an accusing finger at another neighbor, the elderly Nancy Evans with her black cat.

A home remedy was attempted on the Hildebrand porch, which involved taking various items, putting them into a sack and then pounding them and cutting them with an axe. Despite all of their exertions, Mrs. Evans was still very much alive and no doubt shaking her head at what goofy neighbors she had.

Obviously, there was bad blood between Mrs. Evans and her next-door neighbors. At first, the adolescent girls claimed that they saw Mrs. Evans talking to her feline companion. This does not make sense today (after all, everyone who owns pet talks to it), but at the time, it was a serious charge. A lonely old woman would probably talk to her cat a great deal. It did not mean that she actually expected the animal to answer her. But in witchcraft cases, logic is the first casualty.

The mention of an animal with extraordinary powers was vital to the case, as this toxic accusation fit right into the convictions of the era. Witchcraft belief at the time stated that the devil would send animals to his servants to act as familiars. History demonstrated that the mere appearance of an ordinary animal could be sufficient "evidence" to send an innocent person to the gallows.

During the English Civil War a century earlier, a lawyer named Matthew Hopkins, the dreaded Witchfinder General, scoured the eastern English countryside making a good living by sending innocent women to the gallows—and in at least one instance, to be burned alive at the stake. Unlike the more famous Spanish Inquisition, Hopkins's method of torture was to force the accused, usually an elderly woman, to remain awake for long periods of time. If the victim started to nod off, as she invariably would, she would be walked around. After a number of hours of this and constant questioning, her mental resistance would be worn down. During this torture, the sudden appearance of any animal, even so much as a common mouse from behind a stone in the hearth, was sufficient evidence that the accused was a witch. Inevitably, the woman would be sent to her death.

It was on this same convoluted line of reasoning that Mrs. Evans, harmlessly speaking to her black cat, was now suspected of a capital crime.

Just as in Salem, as the girls saw that their wild accusations were taken seriously—and that they were given attention they no doubt craved from their family and community—their charges became even more dramatic. They then stated that they saw strange things floating around in the air at the Evans house.

These wild accusations became local gossip. People started to look at old Mrs. Evans a little differently. Things became even more serious when a man from Pennsylvania wisely stated that what he saw in Bethel was very similar to a case of demonic attack he had witnessed in his home state. Idle chatter was now evidence.

Nancy Evans was being shunned by her neighbors and complained to the justice of the peace, Houton Clarke. However, the neighbors had also been complaining to him concerning the possible presence of a witch in their midst. The situation was becoming quite dangerous, and now this poor man had quite a problem on his hands.

He saw the ominous parallels between what was playing out before him and the shameful Salem witch trials. He also had a very real legal problem in front of him. Witchcraft was definitely considered to be a capital crime in holy scripture. However, his office was to enforce the laws of Ohio, and in the state, there was no legal statute against witchcraft.

Fearful of a witch hysteria that could result in a mass of executions, he decided on a unique method of settling the matter once and for all. He convinced people that if Mrs. Evans was indeed a witch, then the power and sanctity of the Bible would have greater weight than her sinful, devil-ridden

The danger of witchcraft accusations the 1692 Salem Witch Trials. Twenty people were executed, nineteen hanged and one crushed to death. *Library of Congress*

body. Thus all that they had to do to prove the matter conclusively was to weigh Mrs. Evans against a Bible.

On a late Saturday morning, the accused woman was dutifully taken to a low spot over purifying water. (Today, it is still a low spot in the road, which is located near a Speedway gas station.) Nearby was a grain mill, which supplied a large scale that suited the purpose of the weighing.

On one side of the scale was placed the holy and infallible word of God. On the other, the elderly woman accused by her neighbors of being a witch. Which was heavier?

The absurd procedure was given as much dignity as possible. Nancy Evans, before being placed on the scale like a sack of feed, was thoroughly searched by two elderly women. They both proclaimed that she was not cheating—there were no hidden weights concealed on her that might literally tip the scales of justice.

She was then helped up the crude steps and weighed against the word of God.

Mrs. Evans was heavier than the book—a great deal heavier, in fact. The people were delighted. A public announcement stated, "Nancy Evans, by the evidence of the Holy Bible and in the eyes of the good people here assembled, your innocence is hereby and for all times publicly declared." As if to distract the crowd from any spontaneous acts of violence, a small band immediately began to play music. These were not church hymns but rather popular tunes of the day.

The witch trial had turned into a spontaneous barn dance.

The Hildebrands could say nothing, for it had been genuinely proven for all to see that the woman they had accused was not in any way a witch.

Not only was she not a sorceress, but she was also apparently quite ahead of her time. Angry, and probably a little damp, as the scale had been placed over a pond, she immediately found an attorney and took her former accusers to court, suing them for all of the public humiliation she had to endure. She won the case easily and collected a little over twenty-one dollars.

Understandably disgusted with the people of Bethel who would allow her to be subjected to such nonsense, Mrs. Evans packed up her black cat and other belongings and moved to Hamersville, Ohio. Not long afterward, she died peacefully.

There is a story that the Hildebrands became pariahs among the neighbors, and one account even states that they were run out of town in the classic tradition on a rail.

The comical activities in Bethel would be good for a laugh, except for one slight problem: accusations of witchcraft were very serious matters in the early days of this country. It is hard to say exactly how many people lost their lives because they were accused of practicing the devil's arts. Sometimes these dark proceedings were in remote locations, and over the years, the details became lost or almost invariably mixed with local folklore. There is only the memory that something terrible had taken place.[45]

The very first reported case of witchcraft being officially examined by a court (that we can be certain of) was in Jamestown, Virginia, in 1622. "Goodwife" Joan Wright was a healer and a midwife—a common theme for many accused witches. Despite helping her neighbors, she was accused of bewitching cattle, correctly predicting the deaths of four people and even using witchcraft to kill an infant.

Wright was arraigned for the crime, but there is no surviving record of a trial. However, reports do show that later, for an unspecified reason, she was fined the amount of one hundred pounds of tobacco.

Other women were not so lucky. The first actual witchcraft mania occurred not in Salem but in Connecticut, a state that seemed to harbor an undue number of witches.

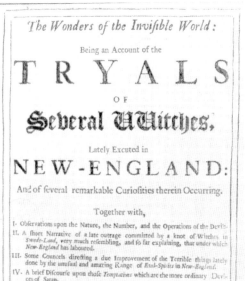

Above: A brighter side of Bethel, home of the future general and president Grant. *From the collection of the Public Library of Cincinnati and Hamilton County.*

Left: Cotton Mather was a major force behind the Salem Witch Trials. In 1689, he had a Catholic woman executed for witchcraft. *Library of Congress.*

The list of early American executions for sorcery is long. Among this group is Margaret Jones, a healing woman who was hanged in Boston in 1648; Mrs. Kendal in Cambridge, Massachusetts, in 1651; and Lydia Gilbert in Winsor, Connecticut, in 1654. At the other end of the continent, three men were hanged for witchcraft in Santa Fe, while more than forty others were arrested. In Mexico City, some people were put on trial for witchcraft by the inquisition but managed to escape—only to be killed by Apaches.

One can add to this list the number of people who were arrested on spurious charges of practicing witchcraft who were scourged but not executed. Included here would be William Harding of Virginia, who in 1656, was sentenced to ten lashes and banishment. Numerous others, mostly women, were imprisoned under horrific conditions and tortured to secure a confession. Even those who were acquitted of the charges would find that their lives were completely ruined, and the stain of the accusation would follow them for the rest of their days.[46]

No, there was nothing at all funny or light about being charged with witchcraft in the early days. Bethel's Nancy Evans was extremely fortunate to have a judge who had sense and a moral compass. As we can see from the historical record, it could have ended very badly indeed.

However, while the one and only legal trial for witchcraft may have ended in Ohio in 1805, belief in witchcraft had not gone away. If the law wasn't going to help good Christian people deal with the servants of Satan, then it was obviously necessary to take matters into their own hands.

BELIEF IN WITCHES AND THE ERADICATION THEREOF

She came—she came—and the quivering flame
Sank and died in the fire.
It never was lit again on my hearth
Since I hurried across the floor,
To lift her over the threshold, and let her in at the door.
—Mary Elizabeth Coleridge, "The Witch"

There has always been a major problem in dealing with witches. These minions of Satan would practice their dark arts alone, usually in the dead of night in such lonely places as cemeteries or underneath gallows and often in the privacy of their cabin. Unlike other crimes, there is never any direct physical evidence to link the perpetrator to the victim. How then does one go about protecting oneself against a witch? How does one capture a criminal whose crime is committed in complete secrecy and does not leave a single trace?

Superstitions die hard and slowly. Despite the change in the beliefs of society, the conviction of the reality of witchcraft was still prevalent. Along with this potentially dangerous belief came new methods to determine if certain people who lived on the outskirts of society were in communion with the devil. There were always a few well-intentioned people of varying degrees of sanity ready to take it on themselves and combat the evil that they perceived to be attacking them.

To fill this need, a new breed of charlatan rose up—the person known colloquially as the witch doctor. Unlike the impression given in old Tarzan movies, this was a person who was supposed to be an expert on the matters of witchcraft and could—for a fee—assist in finding out who the culprit was and tell the victim how to deal with the problem.

There can be no doubt that due to the "wisdom" of these witch doctors, there were many false accusations of witches. One can further speculate that some of these allegations even led to violence—acts that were never recorded. Of the few such cases that have survived the test of time is this curious tale from Cumminsville near Cincinnati's Mill Creek in 1814.

Back when this region was known as Wooden Shoe Hollow due to the number of German immigrants who made their living by the Mill Creek, there was a farmer whose name sadly was not recorded. The chronicler of the early history of the region, Henry B. Teetor, merely states that he was "one of our most wealthy and respectable farmers on Mill creek."[47] The unidentified farmer's greatest claim to fame in the new community was his herd of fine horses—the envy of his neighbors.

A rather romanticized depiction of the Mill Creek in the Cumminsville area. *From the collection of the Public Library of Cincinnati and Hamilton County.*

However, one by one, the horses began to get sick and die from ailments that even an experienced breeder such as he had never seen before. The logical solution would be to summon the best veterinarian available, but this farmer did not think that way. It became apparent to him that he was suffering the predations not of any natural disease but of a curse put on his prized horses by some enemy practicing witchcraft.

Desperate to find a solution to this problem, he sought the advice of one of these witch doctors, a person who was supposedly renowned for his intimate knowledge of the ways of witches. This person alone could give him the necessary information to identify the sorceress and stop the sickness that was devastating his herd of horses.

He paid this man and received the information he was looking for. He was told to take a cauldron and boil a certain mixture of herbs and mix it with a large number of needles and pins. He was assured that boiling this concoction in great heat "would produce great mental and bodily distress"[48] in the witch who was causing the problem. Once the strange mixture started to boil, he should watch for the witch to show herself.

He followed the instructions to the letter, and as the concoction was boiling away, he stood in the door of his house and watched carefully. Sure enough, his own daughter-in-law suddenly appeared, running as fast as she could with a bucket and filling it with cool water from the stream.

Feeling assured that he had found his witch, he went to his son and accused him and his wife of destroying his horses. A fierce argument broke out, but the old man would not back down. Infuriated, he ordered the family to leave his property as soon as possible. Angry and insulted, they did.

Unfortunately, his horses were still dying of this mysterious disease. With his daughter-in-law gone, he now tried to figure out who else could be the witch—perhaps there was more than one. Maybe his daughter-in-law was just an amateur witch who had gone to a more experienced sorceress to start the process.

Figuring that all witches were elderly women, he found the only one possible—a feeble old woman named Mrs. Garrison. This sick old woman lived nearly ten miles away and had little to no contact with him, but as she was old and female, he figured she had to be the witch. He let word slip to some close friends about this, and soon gossip was spreading throughout the district. Now tongues were wagging, and people started to regard old Mrs. Garrison as a witch.

But how could he do away with her legally? The wealthy farmer had been informed that the best way to destroy a witch was to shoot her with silver bullets. Of course, for him to just shoot the old woman would certainly result in a charge of first-degree murder. It would be a hard sell for a jury.

Happily for him, this was not necessary. He reasoned that he could just as easily make an image of her and simply shoot the image. There was certainly no law against that. Even better, he could reverse the spell by shooting one of the cursed horses. That way, the power of his counter-magic would work its way backward to the source.

As silver bullets are not easily acquired, it is assumed that he melted some buttons from his military uniform. Fashioning this into a bullet, he picked one of his prize horses who was dying from the mysterious ailment and dutifully shot it dead.

Sure enough, it was not long before old Mrs. Garrison died. Of course, she was quite old and not in the best of health to begin with. Henry Teetor, chronicling the strange event, noted, "Poor Mrs. Garrison died, the experiment was declared to be successful, and the experimenter believed to his death, that his silver bullet killed the poor old woman. However, that may be, his slanderous report had a great effect on her health, and no doubt hastened her death."[49]

Unfortunately, the account abruptly ends there. It is never revealed whether the man's sick horses recovered or others in the herd stopped becoming ill after his bit of magic.

In 1828, there was a horrific case of witchcraft—one that sadly involved cruelty to an animal. This occurred in Lawrence County in the southeastern corner of the state. Word came out of this rural locale that there was a problem with witchcraft. There were a number of cases of witches harming various people in the area, causing illness among not only the animals but also the people. *The Historical Collections of Ohio* lists a number of these cases, but once again does not supply the names of the victims.

One of the first of these victims was a horse with a "drooping appearance." As in the Cumminsville case, it was determined that the steed was not the victim of any natural horse disease but rather a spell cast by local witches.

When a young woman became mysteriously ill, a witch doctor was sent for. This shaman unsurprisingly diagnosed the problem as a curse of witchcraft. He then performed a kind of exorcism, informing the family that he was driving out the witches or, more precisely, the evil spirits that were inside of the girl. He further stated that there were indeed witches in the area—one in particular was an elderly woman. He added that the only way that she could be defeated would be killing her.

There was, according to his wisdom on the subject, another method of removing the evil spirits from an animal—burning the cursed creature alive. The witch doctor then pocketed his fee and left the area, leaving the family to ponder if they should take this horrific course of action. Sadly, they followed his instructions.

The farmer who had paid the witch doctor to remove the spirits from one of his horses was called away on business. While he was gone, the family cow started to act up. At first, the farmer's wife believed that the animal had rabies; however, when the farmer returned, he stated that the spirits that the witch doctor exorcized from the horse had now returned, as the Bible states they will.[50] These evil spirits had now found refuge in the family cow.

They decided to follow the witch doctor's advice and end this once and for all by burning the animal alive. At first, the more rational neighbors laughed at the farmer, thinking he was foolish. However, a bit reluctantly, they helped him secure the poor beast to a tree. With a generous supply of kindling, both the tree and the strapped-down bovine were set ablaze.

Afterward, the family believed that the matter was finally ended, and they could be at peace, knowing that they had secured a victory over the witches. However, rather than going to bed, the farmer said that the family should remain up and alert and keep careful watch out of the window at the spot where the embers of the bonfire were still glowing.

The family thought that he was a bit mad, which was also the general consensus of the neighbors. It had been a hard day, and they wanted to go to sleep. Undaunted by their protests, he assured them that if this was indeed a question of witchcraft, then the witches would come to the fire at night.

Hours and hours passed in the dark as members of the family took their shifts sitting by the window and looking out at the glowing pile of ash. Suddenly, one of them called out. The farmer and the rest of his family rushed to the window and saw a frightening spectacle.

In the glow of the embers, they could see two women having quite a celebration at the place of the immolation. They were dancing around and leaping over the remnants of the pyre. Every so often, they would grab hold of a brand and toss it to the other or throw it up in the air.

After that bizarre occurrence, there was no further problem with witchcraft in the area. The ceremony, as cruel as it was, seemed to satisfy them as a kind of dark sacrifice to the devil and his loyal servants.

It is interesting to note that the eerie festivities commencing over the place of burning harkens back to the ancient days of Europe. The curious practice of witches leaping over the fiery pile is eerily reminiscent of both Celtic and

Teutonic witchcraft traditions. On the feast of Samhain, what we know today as Halloween, and in central Europe on the springtime night of Beltane (the German *Walpurgisnacht*), young men would prove their bravery—and impress the girls—by leaping over a bonfire. However, when the festivities ended, everyone had to rush back to their homes, fearful of encountering anyone or anything on the road, for the witches were out on that eve. Often, they would run off shouting, "Der Teufel hat das Nachsehen!" or "Let the devil take the hindmost!"[51]

Just across the state line in Indiana, the Hoosiers were spared the embarrassment and bloodshed of witch trials, but they were not free from the dangers of witchcraft and the curious efforts of common people to stop their magic. One instance from the earliest pioneer days testifies to this.

One of the most bizarre cases in Indiana was from the early 1830s in Gibson County. Gossip was spreading through the countryside that a young couple, Jonas Griffy and his wife, Casway, were attempting to find a way to melt silver coins and combine them with lead.

People saw this, and soon, the pair was suspected of being a couple of counterfeiters. They explained in confidence that they were not trying to make their own coin of the realm but merely wanted to kill a witch. Apparently, "they said there was an old woman who lived near them in Martin County who was a terror to all the country round. She did not fear anything, would ride without a bridle and saddle the wildest, unbroken horse and would fight any man. She had nearly killed two of their neighbors in a fight."[52] Folk belief assured them that the only way to put an end to such a terror was to shoot the witch with a bullet made of silver.

This unnamed witch committed the crime most often associated with witches: stealing milk and making cows run dry. However, unlike most other similar accusations, this particular witch was apparently caught in the act:

The old witch did not have any cows, but always had plenty of milk and butter. "We tried" said they, "many ways to find out how the cows were milked, but did not succeed until one morning one of our women went up to the old witch's house and saw her doing something with a towel which was hanging in a small window." While the witch's back was turned she determined to find out what she was doing. She first stuck a pin in the towel and named it for one of our cows. Then she took hold of the fringe and commenced to milk it as if she were milking a cow.[53]

She did this over and over, naming another person's cow and apparently receiving the milk that should have gone to the rightful owners.

The witch also had the power to shape-shift and soon held the area in terror of a huge black cat that would maraud the countryside at night. However, this soon became a one-eared cat: "Finally old Mr. McCoy, one of our people, saw the cat go into his room. He closed the door and armed himself with an axe. Opening the door a little ways to let the cat run out, which it did, he cut off one of its ears. The next morning one of our women went over to see the old lady and found her in bed with a bandage on her head."[54] The witch snuck back to McCoy's place the next night and stole her ear back. The next time she was seen, the ear had grown back and looked the same as it always had.

Salem, Ohio, is located in the northeast area of the state, straddling the counties of Mahoning and Columbiana. The area has a curious claim to fame, as it was the home of the famous disc jockey Alan Freed—the man who coined the term *rock and roll* in 1951.

Founded in 1806, the city name is a shortened form of "Jerusalem." Inhabited originally by Quakers, it was a bastion of civil rights, a major station along the Underground Railroad and, in 1850, the host of a convention for women's rights.

The witchcraft case occurred in 1893 and was a matter of hysteria that easily could have turned deadly. It all began with a farmer named Howard Hughes digging a well on his land. He had dug quite deep—far past where he believed he should have struck water, but all that he had for his labors was exhaustion and a rather large pile of dirt. Feeling that this was not natural, he decided that sorcery must be to blame.

He made a trip to nearby Alliance to consult a man known as Doctor Huff. This man was more witch doctor than medical practitioner. He was a medium (by this time spiritualism was becoming very popular) and was supposedly quite knowledgeable about the world of the spirits and those who have dealings with them.

The doctor put on a good performance, visiting the dry hole Hughes had dug and tossing numerous "magical" powders in. When the ceremony was over, he declared conclusively that the well was indeed dry due to the machinations of witchcraft. He even went so far as to identify the culprit: a man named William (in some accounts he is listed as Jacob) Culp.

Culp had committed what may be considered the greatest of sins—he was wealthy and successful; thus, people were envious of his good fortune. Like many others in the area, he was a German immigrant. He had come to the New World as a boy and settled in this region. He took up farming and, through hard work, became rather prosperous.

Just before the Civil War began in 1860, he married a woman named Hannah. With this union, he became the stepfather to her two children. Later on, he took in his mother-in-law, Mary Loop, and his disabled brother-in-law, Ephraim. Mary Loop died afterward, and for some reason, his sister-in-law Sadie began to suspect William of witchcraft. To make matters worse, around 1887, Hannah died. Soon after that tragedy, Culp married a much younger woman.

Thanks to Sadie's suspicions and her venomous tongue, whispers of witchcraft quickly spread throughout the locale. Inevitably, any problem that befell the people of Salem was now blamed on the nocturnal spells of William Culp. When Norman Breen's cattle became sick and died, it was thought to have been the result of a curse by his wealthy neighbor. One of his relatives suffered a broken leg, and this too was considered magical.

Things were quickly getting out of hand. Soon almost any misfortune that would befall people of the community was blamed on the diabolic designs of the sorcerer Culp.

The accusations became more prevalent and vicious. Soon there was another accuser, none other than Culp's former sister-in-law, the gossiping Sadie Loop. Emboldened by the opinion of the neighbors, she now publically charged that Culp had murdered his wife.

While there was no legal remedy for the crime of witchcraft, there was a spiritual method of dealing with the problem. A trial in the local Hart Methodist Episcopal Church began, and William Culp was officially accused and tried for the sin—but not the crime—of witchcraft. The judge was to be the pastor, Reverend Smith.

However, things did not work out as the accusers had hoped. Another member of the congregation, Homer B. Shelton, had complained in a formal indictment that Sadie was immoral in making false accusations of witchcraft. Despite what the complainants believed to be overwhelming evidence of the dark arts, the verdict went the other way. Mr. Culp was permitted to remain a member of good standing in the congregation. However, just as had happened in Bethel, it was those who had made the wild accusations who faced punishment. Sadie Loop, Norman Breen and Howard Hughes were all expelled from the congregation.

It is curious to note that one of the victims of this crime was the church itself. It was soon abandoned, and today all that is left of it is a small cemetery on Route 45.[55]

In November 1845, J.L. Wilson delivered his famous sermon on witchcraft at the First Presbyterian Church in Cincinnati. The sermon was so popular that it was later printed as a twenty-three-page pamphlet and sold. Copies of it are still available for purchase today. Along with traditional witches, he also included such groups as Roman Catholics, Shakers, Mormons, the New Jerusalem Church and mesmerists. His greatest ire was directed toward the eighteenth-century mystic Emanuel Swedenborg, who he referred to as the "prince of modern necromancers."[56]

One reviewer took issue with the reverend's all-encompassing view of the nature of witchcraft, complaining that the serious charge was being used as a blanket indictment against mainstream Christianity. His criticism was on solid ground. Wilson had stated that "Mormonism is simply an unprincipled movement of artful deceivers, whose dupes are sufficiently ready to be deceived. What is new of Shakerism and Mesmerism is not true, and what is true is not new. A considerable share of the phenomena in both these, is referable to the nervous system; the residue a sheer imposture of men who begin dupes and end deceivers. In this category I place the whole horde of neurologists, mesmerists, clairvoyants, &c."[57]

The reverend opened his sermon by informing the congregation that the average person does not appreciate the gravity of the sin:

> It [witchcraft] *is the name of an offence which the inspired writer has ranked with idolatry, murder and drunkenness. About this crime, however, very little is said among us....Witchcraft is scarcely named in the pulpit, seldom noticed in our public journals, and if mentioned in conversation it seems only for the purpose of turning the subject into ridicule, and making people believe that no such crime was ever committed. If witchcraft was one of the works of the flesh, which excluded men from heaven, in former times—in what some suppose to be the purest age of the church—may it not do so now? It is surely not a thing impossible.*[58]

He further clarified the definition of the sin by stating that witchcraft includes "divination, enchantment, necromancy, soothsaying, sorcery, exorcism, and every variety of device by which these arts are practiced, whether it be called charm, spell, or some forms of superstition, denominated religious ceremonies."[59]

He defined witches as being those with "the skill and power of doing something, which is not accomplished by the ordinary laws of nature."[60]

Essentially, he stated that witches had the power to contradict or bend the laws of cause and effect.

After deriding Catholics, Shakers and Mormons, he returned to the mystical by discussing the occult teachings of Emanuel Swedenborg. He began by discussing the new practice of hypnotism, at the time known as mesmerism:

> So far as they practice their art, it tends either to infidelity or "Swedenborgianism." This is necromancy—the power of conversing with the dead and familiar spirits—the very art practiced [sic] by the woman of Endor who gave Saul an opportunity of talking with Samuel. Emanuel Swedenborg was evidently the Prince of modern necromancers, and to him the mesmerizers claim a strong affinity. If we can believe them the internal man can leave the external, and after travelling to other worlds and holding converse with the dead, return again and inhabit his former dwelling; neither time nor space nor distance oppose any obstacle to such somnambulists.[61]

He continued his criticism of Swedenborg:

> Having denied almost every important doctrine of the Christian religion, and having devised a scheme of salvation foreign from the plan laid down in the New Testament, he was evidently given up of God to strong delusion and became one of the greatest dupes to evil spirits. He thought himself able constantly to see and converse with spirits and angels, both in the body and out of the body. While we readily allow that there have been many mere pretenders to witchcraft, who have imposed upon the ignorant and credulous by arts of deception, we must as cordially admit that there have been and still are true practitioners of this wonderful art. There can be no counterfeits where there is nothing true. The gospel of Christ, then, is the remedy—the only remedy for the evils of Witchcraft. Men have been given up to delusion, because they believe not the truth; let them now renounce their false systems and return to the Lord who is merciful. Under the gospel dispensation, God has promised to cut off all witchcrafts…by the conversion or destruction of all practitioners of Witchcraft.[62]

Destruction of all practitioners? These were dangerous words, for there is always a person whose grip on reality is not as firm as society would appreciate.

Even on the very edge of the twentieth century, the age-old belief and fear of witches refused to die. In 1897, on Queen City Avenue on the west side of Cincinnati, a woman was arrested for her personal crusade to rid the world of witches. A woman named Mary Becker was taken into custody to appear before Squire Winkler. Her crime was threatening her neighbor Magdalen Grow. Mrs. Becker was convinced that her neighbor was a witch, and even went so far as to threaten to burn her. The reasons for this curious conclusion were never given.

In modern parlance, it would appear that Mrs. Becker was a few bricks shy of a load. Thankfully, she was stopped before she could strike her match.

The twentieth century did not end the belief and fear of witches. A sad and head-scratching case of suspected witchcraft murder resulted in the death of one woman in Cleveland in 1935. Mrs. Mathilda Waldman suspected that Ida Cooper, the owner of a small grocery store, was making her ill with witchcraft and was even sending fireballs into her home. Mrs. Waldman went to the grocery store and demanded that Mrs. Cooper stop abusing her with sorcery and sign a paper that she had written promising to stop hexing her.

Of course, she was met with a hearty laugh. Mrs. Cooper should have signed it.

Mrs. Waldman returned not with a piece of paper but with a pistol. Mrs. Cooper was shot dead. Waldman tried to flee the scene, but Cooper's sons chased her down. When the judge asked her how she felt now that she killed Mrs. Cooper, Mrs. Waldman simply stated that she was relieved.

In August 1964, there was another instance of a witchcraft trial in Ohio in Cincinnati. However, this one was not for summoning spirits but rather a matter of practicing medicine without bothering to go to medical school or securing any manner of pharmacist license.

Lorenzo W. Williams appeared before Judge A.L. Luebbers, charged with practicing medicine without a license. The court was no doubt entertained by the appearance of the defendant, who was wearing earrings (something few men did in 1964), a large rosary and various amulets about his neck. In fashion sense, he was about four years ahead of his time.

While this was not a common case heard before a municipal court, it is interesting to note that this was actually the second time that Mr. Williams had stood before a judge to face the same accusation. Almost a full year earlier, in July 1963, he had appeared before Judge Wood on the charge of practicing medicine without a license. That time, the judge was lenient—he gave Williams probation but warned him to not practice any kind of medical work or distribute any mixtures that would be considered medicine. Apparently, Williams did not comprehend the message and went back to his old ways.

In the summer of 1964, Williams was the proprietor of the Hindu East Indian Products Company at 653 West Court Street, located at the intersection of Cutter Street in the West End. On July 17, the police raided the small establishment and arrested Williams once again for practicing medicine without a license. Making their way through a bizarre room of exotic items that could be found at a low-class flea market, they found their erstwhile wizard sitting over his cauldron—a six-quart pot of noxious liquid boiling away as he put in a seemingly random mixture of herbs.

The Hindu sorcerer with the distinctly non-Indian name did not know that a few days earlier, his establishment had been visited by Cecil Scott, an investigator for the Medical Board of Ohio. This undercover visit had been spurred on by the receipt of a complaint from one of Williams's patients, a man named William Stamp.

Stamp, who lived on Lincoln Park Drive (now Ezzard Charles Drive), was a painter by profession and had been hired to do some work in the Hindu East Indian Products Shop. Amid his labor, he began to talk to Williams and casually stated that he had a terrible pain in his back and shoulders. This was music to Williams's ears. He sold the painter a bottle of strange tonic for the princely sum of one dollar and the promise to perform more work for him (this time without being paid).

It turned out to be a very bad bargain. Williams may have been an excellent salesman, but he was not a very good pharmacist. Stamp took the mixture faithfully but received no relief from his pains. Finally, the concoction became so fetid that the odor prevented him from poisoning himself any further.

But by now the damage was done. He was rushed to General Hospital, where he told the story to astonished doctors. The noxious mixture had severely damaged him, particularly his hip. He had no choice but to endure surgery. The hospital immediately contacted the medical board, prompting the undercover investigation by Cecil Scott and the appearance of Williams in court.

Facing familiar charges, Williams declared that he had never given any medical diagnosis and did not distribute medicine. What he did not know when saying so was that Scott had done an undercover investigation of his curious shop. Williams was confident that the evidence against him had been swallowed, but thankfully, his "patient" had not finished all of the mixture. The curious concoction had been taken to a laboratory and analyzed.

In the testimony of the trial, Cincinnati's official bacteriologist, Oto P. Behrer, stated that he had examined the remnants of the medicine Williams gave to Stamp. He testified that there were so many different forms of bacteria present in the mixture that he could not even begin to count them all.

The judge had heard enough. With a sharp bang of the gavel, Judge Luebbers sentenced Williams to a $100 fine and thirty days as a guest of the county in the workhouse.

Williams, angry at the undercover surveillance of his weird business, declared in a loud voice that he would have his revenge on those who persecuted him so unjustly. He announced to everyone in earshot that he would use his dark magical powers to place a hex on the investigator.

However, just like his medicines, there was no appreciable effect on the victim of his curse. When laughing reporters later asked him about this apparent discrepancy, the humiliated wizard simply replied that these things take a bit of time.[63]

This case is certainly not the only one of its kind in Ohio. In 1929, the Cleveland police charged in on Sylvester Williams. The supposed sorcerer had been fasting for some time and was emaciated. He stated that he was just about to go into a trance but was interrupted. The Cleveland police believed that he was part of a "voodoo cult" that had been practicing in the city and was connected with the murder of a man who was found decapitated in a closet.[64]

So much for the madness, comedy and tragedy of battling the witches of Ohio. Now that we have seen the hunters, let us look at their prey.

4

OHIO WITCHES
AND THEIR WAYS

We shall see that at which dogs howl in the dark,
and that at which cats prick up their ears after midnight.
—H.P. Lovecraft

It was the spring of 1898. The place was Lawson Post Office in Raleigh County, across the river from Ohio in West Virginia. It was, as in many cases of sorcery, the familiar scenario of people believing that they were cursed.

Griffith Jarrell was a typical farmer in the mountainous area. However, four of his children, a ten-year-old boy and three daughters, suddenly became ill with a mysterious disease. Sadly, the chronicler did not include any of the symptoms of the illness other than to say that no one in the area had experienced such a disease before.

After consultation, it was decided that the children were not suffering from any physical disease but instead were the victims of witchcraft. Suspicion immediately fell on two people. One of these was Mrs. Lukens, an old woman who seemed to be right out of Hansel and Gretel, who lived alone in a log cabin deep in the woods. The other suspect was a man named Mr. Blizzard, who also lived by himself in a wooded area. Why either of these outcasts would want to harm the Jarrell children was never explained.

After consulting some homegrown experts on witchcraft, it was recommended that effigies of both Mrs. Lukens and Mr. Blizzard be fashioned and then shot with silver bullets. This was supposedly the only way to break the spell.

Small mannequins representing each of the suspected witches were fashioned. When they had finished their work, a group of local men gathered and, after a quick prayer, loaded their hunting rifles and proceeded to shoot at the two dolls. The one representing Mr. Blizzard was shot to pieces immediately.

However, the doll that was supposed to be Mrs. Lukens was not shot once, even though it was at the exact same range as the other effigy—and those old mountain boys didn't miss, certainly not an unmoving target at that range. The men lowered their rifles and looked at one another in amazement. Something unnatural was apparently preventing the bullets from hitting the doll, and everyone concluded that the something was witchcraft.

Convinced that they had found the sorceress living in their midst, the men then made their way deep into the woods to search for Mrs. Lukens. However, before they arrived, she decided that this would be an excellent time to see the world beyond Raleigh County and made a quick change of address. When the angry mob arrived at her cabin, she was nowhere to be seen.

This does invite one interesting question: as she lived alone in a remote location, how did she know that they were coming?

People thought that the sudden departure of the suspected witch would end the problem. But this was not the case. Things became even stranger. A local man, Mr. Wells, condescendingly referred to in the newspaper account as a witch doctor (the traditional Appalachian term for a person knowledgeable in the ways of witches would be *granny witch*, or *gramps witch* in this case), entered the drama. He tried some magical conjurations of his own to solve the problem.

He placed a bottle filled with pins and other sundry items in water and heated it. As the Jarrells and neighbors looked on in amazement, Wells performed an incantation over the procedure and solemnly announced that the water would not boil before the witch who put the spell on the family made an appearance. Wells said that person would want to borrow something. (We shall see this feature of witches borrowing items numerous times in this study.)

It was all nonsense, of course. The laws of physics assure us that when water is heated to a certain temperature, it will boil. That makes perfect sense, except for one small thing: even though the liquid became quite hot, it didn't bubble in the least. It eventually did, but just before the water boiled, who should come knocking on the door but old Mr. Blizzard himself. Of course, true to Mr. Wells's prophecy, he wanted to borrow something.

He came very close to receiving a great deal of buckshot instead of the requested item. Enraged, Mr. Jarrell was in the process of grabbing his shotgun when the heat suddenly caused the bottle to explode, sending shards of shrapnel, pins and whatever else was in the concoction all around the room. In the confusion, the suspected wizard escaped with his life.

A Presbyterian minister, Dr. Humble, saw the fear gripping his mountain community and knew from history that these things could turn very ugly. He did everything that he could to convince the people that the problems striking the community were from natural causes and not from the diabolic art of witchcraft. His pleas fell on deaf ears. The people in Raleigh County were now certain that they were under attack from the devil and his minions.

Despite the reverend's pious and scientific exertions, matters only became worse. As has happened in numerous witchcraft outbreaks over the centuries, more and more people were affected, or as they believed, cursed. One of these victims was young James Shepherd. Indeed, the infliction was so bad that it ended in James being sent to an asylum.

In desperation, the families involved contacted a second old man skilled in dealing with witches, a Mr. Stover. He examined the sick children and went about the business of performing a spell. It was a difficult process. He informed the parents that it would take nine days to achieve the desired results. According to him, after nine days, all of the children would be better.

However, whether his magic worked or not will never be truly known. By now, word of this wildness had reached Raleigh Court House. The embarrassed government officials had to stop things before the situation got completely out of their control. They sent in Dr. Daniels who, along with Reverend Humble, convinced the families to allow them to take the children to a medical facility where they promised that the youngsters would receive the best care. Finally, the desperate families agreed, and the young people were whisked away to a hospital. Here, as was reported, "The children are all well and hearty, recovering readily under a healthy, moral atmosphere."[65]

While this may seem like a repudiation of the witchcraft beliefs, in a strange way, it actually confirmed them. The witch doctor, Stover, said that they would be better in nine days. He did not say *where* the children would be or how it would come about—only that they would better.

Although the people were ridiculed in many of the big-city newspaper accounts, this case has some interesting points to it. Why could the men, all of whom were experienced hunters and marksmen who could drop a running rabbit, not be able to hit an unmoving doll at close range? How did the witch doctor know that Blizzard would show up before the water boiled, wanting to borrow something? How did Stover know that the children would be better—was it the power of his magic, or did he somehow know that the government would intervene and remove them to a medical facility?

As a side note, there are countless cases of witchcraft in Appalachia in which a practitioner of the black arts goes to a victim wanting to borrow something. If the object, even if it is as small as a cup of sugar or molasses, is given, then according to the folklore, the witch has power over the victim. However, if the request is refused, then the witch's spell cannot work.

These were some of the traditional beliefs that poured into Ohio along with the Appalachians seeking better lives in the big cities of Cleveland, Toledo, Akron, Dayton and Cincinnati. To these new Ohioans, the power of witches was an undisputed fact—and the danger from their dark spells was very real. After all, over the generations, they had seen too much to scoff.

A particularly disturbing case of Gilded Age witchcraft occurred in the small city of Elmwood in March 1885. This may have been a case of a natural death through an undiagnosed disease, a horrible instance of murder by poisoning or, as members of the grieving family suspected, an attack of out-and-out witchcraft. There is evidence to support each one of these suppositions.

North Main Ave., Elmwood Place, Cincinnati.

The small city of Elmwood near Cincinnati at the turn of the century. *From the collection of the Public Library of Cincinnati and Hamilton County.*

Five-year-old Rosa Telljohn died after a bout with a debilitating wasting illness. Sadly, considering the ability of medical science, the death of a young child from disease was not so unusual at this period of history. However, this case was different. Almost immediately, the little girl's father, Henry Telljohn, began to make accusations of witchcraft against the mother of his next-door neighbor. Henry Telljohn worked as a porter in the downtown area. His neighbor, Mr. Hittenberger, worked as a mechanic.

It is important to note that before the tragedy, there was no animosity between the two families. For years, they got along very well. The Telljohn children, including little Rosa, played with the Hittenberger boy, Johnnie.

Mr. Hittenberger's mother, Johanna Ellsworth, lived at Foster's Crossing but was often at the Hittenberger home. She was quite familiar with both families and was well liked by the children as well. However, possibly due to previously losing her own child, she tended to be a bit morbid. One might even speculate that she was a bit mentally ill. She would often speak obsessively about small children dying—the memory of that horrible event from her past clearly eating away at her.

One time, she was a guest in the Telljohn home when she calmly asked a rather inappropriate question of Henry: which of his three children would he be willing to spare?

Most people would be shown the door at this point, but she was the mother of his next-door neighbor, and everyone knew that she was a bit on the eccentric side, so Henry, although shocked and a bit horrified by the question, answered her. "Telljohn replied that he could spare none of them, but if all died he would accept it as God's will."[66]

The elderly woman simply continued her conversation, stating that a child's death was not as bad as that of an adult. From there, the banter returned to more acceptable areas of discussion.

As a kindly elderly woman, a true grandmother, Johanna, for some reason, paid a great deal of attention to little Rosa. This attention may have been unwanted, for in December 1884, the little girl suddenly became very ill.

Johanna was very concerned. It seemed that she was reliving the death of her own child. She visited the little girl every day, tending to her as best as she could, even bringing her homemade soup. At first, little Rosa liked Johanna, as if she was her own grandmother. Then, as her illness worsened, she suddenly began to dislike the elderly woman and wanted nothing to do with her. Now when the old woman brought her soup, she adamantly refused to eat it.

Things became even stranger. Rosa would claim that she could see the shadowy form of "Johnnie's grandmother" wandering around her bedroom at night. The whole time she was making these complaints, she was becoming quite pale and very thin, literally wasting away before their eyes.

The desperate family took her to see Dr. Saffin. Although he examined her thoroughly, he could find no illness in her whatsoever. Rosa was wasting away, and there seemed to be no logical reason for it. Saffin gave them some medicine, but of course, this did no good.

The Telljohn family, frustrated by traditional medical science, decided to employ less orthodox methods to find out what was going on. Desperate to save their daughter's life, they called on Madame Dick, a fortuneteller who was reputed to have great knowledge of all matters occult. This arcane knowledge included the ways of witches and how to stop their spells.

Madame Dick stated that little Rosa was indeed the victim of witchcraft. The fortuneteller then proceeded to describe an elderly woman, a near neighbor, who was both tall and quite slim. Although they had said nothing to Madame Dick about their neighbor's mother, the seer described Johanna Ellsworth perfectly.

The diagnosis did not stop there. The fortuneteller went on to say that this family was always borrowing things. The most important item in this consideration was a clock. This borrowed timepiece was the key to the problem, she emphasized. If the Telljohns wanted their little girl to live, they must go to these people and demand the immediate return of the clock.

Henry marched next door and demanded the return of anything that the Hittenbergers had borrowed over the years. Insulted and enraged, the family gathered everything that had been borrowed and dutifully returned it.

The old woman, who was there at the time, simply watched the proceedings and said nothing about any of this. However, as soon as Henry demanded the return of the clock, the elderly woman was alarmed. She did everything in her power to keep him from taking back the timepiece, complaining that his house had three clocks and her family needed this. In the end, there was no recourse—it was his property, and it was obediently returned.

However, if this indeed was a case of witchcraft, the cure was a tragic case of too little too late. Shortly afterward, Rosa, who by now was little more than a skeleton, developed spinal meningitis and died.

Needless to say, relations between the two neighbors were rather cold after that. Henry did not stop in his denunciation of his next-door neighbors for harboring a witch. Finally, Mr. Hittenberger filed charges for harassment. He appeared before Magistrate Schwab and was ordered to post a two-hundred-dollar bond to guarantee that he would not bother his neighbor any further.

There are three ways of looking at this tragic case. One is that the little girl simply fell sick and died from an unknown illness. Mrs. Hittenberger, angrily defending her family's honor, stated that the little girl had been unwell all winter. Although she was in no way a physician, she stated that the girl died of a brain fever and inflammation of the lungs. She also defended her mother-in-law, stating that the old woman was quite feeble, harmless and certainly had never been accused of anything as horrible as witchcraft in her lifetime.

Despite Mrs. Hittenberger's passionate defense, it should be kept in mind that she was not a doctor, and little Rosa had, in fact, been taken to a physician and thoroughly examined. In those thorough tests, no physical illness could be found, at least consistent with the medical knowledge of the day.

It is possible that the old woman was guilty of a more traditional crime and was actually poisoning Rosa with her "curative" soup. After all, the Greek word *pharmakos* can mean both "poisoner" and "sorcerer." The little girl even stated that the old woman once said to her in private, "Here, Rosa, you eat this and no one else."[67] Recall that Johanna's original question to Henry had been which one of his children he could spare. Rosa was the only one of his three children who she was preparing food for. Apparently, little Rosa suspected this before any of the adults. She turned her affection away from Johanna and went from liking the old woman to being deathly afraid of her.

There is also the bizarre possibility that this was an actual case of witchcraft. There are a number of things to suggest this, including Rosa seeing the shadowy figure of the elderly woman in her room at night. The fortuneteller, Madame Dick, correctly identified the old woman and mentioned borrowing things, particularly the clock. Curiously, this was the one item that the suspected witch did not want to return.

This point is quite significant. As we have seen in many cases of witchcraft, particularly those from the Appalachian region, witches are often identified as wanting to borrow something after they have begun an attack on the victim. Those who counsel the victims always state that these requests, although a terrible breach of etiquette, must be denied for the witch to be defeated and the victim to survive.

It has been said that those people who are under attack by witches will experience strange things in their home, often what is classified as poltergeist phenomena. This is what occult writer Dion Fortune refers to as a psychic attack, manifested by strange smells and sounds and sometimes seeing apparitions. Whether one is dealing with a poltergeist, the machinations of a witch or simply some unexplained natural phenomena can be quite a mystery.[68]

In 1879, there was a case of a family frightened by the sudden appearance of poltergeist activity and phantoms. On Barr Street in Cincinnati, a man lived with his wife, daughter and elderly mother. The problem is that all of a sudden, the lodgings appeared to be quite haunted. There were cold spots, the gas flame would inexplicably become blue (evidence of the presence of a supernatural entity according to folk belief), they heard various strange sounds and closet doors were opening by themselves. Worst of all was a massive sound going through one of the bedrooms, like a company of spectral soldiers marching. It was described poetically: "As if a procession of plow boys with double soled boots were walking straight through the room."[69] One can only imagine what that would sound like. Some thought that it sounded like an entire column of soldiers making their way through the bedroom.

This particular room was the sleeping quarters of the man's mother. Although she had lived a long while and had seen many things in her life, this was too much for her. She fled from her haunted bedroom and took to sleeping in the bed with her son and his wife, neither of whom were particularly happy with the new arrangements.

The neighbors were consulted. They believed that this was the work of a witch and strongly recommended calling in a medium and conducting a séance in the apartment. However, the tortured family did not want to have any dealings with spiritualists and sought other remedies.

A skeptical newspaper reporter examined the apartment and found that the shutters were broken, and if the wind was just right, they would make a thumping sound. This was offered as a rather pathetic explanation, although it can hardly account for the fact that this phenomena happened nearly every single night, even when there was no wind. Unless that particular building was in a constant hurricane, it would certainly not be a plausible explanation for the very loud noise of the aforementioned plowboys doing Russian folk dances on the bedroom floor. Furthermore, an elderly woman would not willingly leave her privacy and invade the marriage bed of her son and his wife. Obviously, something far out of the ordinary was taking place in that apartment.

Ohio is proud of its nickname the Birthplace of Presidents. What is not generally known is that one of these chief executives' wives was being guided by a witch. There are some very strange things reported connected with President Warren G. Harding, owner of the newspaper the *Marion Star*.

Harding's administration was among the most corrupt ever known. A shady group of characters known in the press as the Ohio Gang was involved in numerous slimy practices in the early days of Prohibition.

Harding was quite a partier. Not only did he have two mistresses and an illegitimate child, he was also an avid gambler. He once placed a bet at a card game using the White House china as the stakes. He lost the hand and dutifully packed up and shipped away the White House china, even though he was not really the owner of the priceless tableware.

It may surprise people to know that the Harding administration was the only one to have a witch involved. Mrs. Harding, known informally as the Duchess, was, like Mary Todd Lincoln, an avid believer in spiritualism. She had even visited Camp Chesterfield in Indiana, a haven for spiritualists. A chair on display in the Harding home museum has a crescent moon carved into it, which was used by a medium to contact the dead.

The Duchess had her own seer, a mysterious woman born Marcia Champney and later known as Little Olive and then Madame Marcia. This American sibyl would sometimes be sneaked into the White House using the back stairs frequented only by the servants.

The witch predicted not only the Teapot Dome scandal that would ruin Harding's legacy but also that he would die in office. At the very beginning of the administration, she told Mrs. Harding that the term would be tumultuous and that he would not survive. When the lid was blown off of the Teapot Dome scandal, President Harding decided to change his ways. He took a trip to Alaska, but on the trip, he died, just as the witch had predicted.

There is a great deal of supernatural activity connected to the death of this president. One of the items on display in his Marion, Ohio home is a clock placed on the wall by a staircase. The clock stopped at the moment of his death and has not been running ever since.

As Teapot Dome scandal erupted, there was yet another omen of the president's imminent death. The Hardings had received the present of a finch. The Duchess absolutely hated birds, but as the present was from a powerful Republican ally of her husband, she had no choice but to keep it.

When the Hardings left for the ill-fated trip to Alaska, she covered the cage. However, once in the darkness, the bird began to sing. Mrs. Harding believed that this was a sure sign that her seer's prophecy would soon come true and her husband would die.

The Duchess, Florence Harding, pins a rose on her husband's lapel. Mrs. Harding had her own witch as an adviser. *Library of Congress.*

She was right. The president became ill on the journey and died on August 2, 1923, in San Francisco. To make matters even more mysterious, the honor guard at his funeral was irritated by mysterious rocks being thrown at them, although no one saw anyone actually tossing the stones.[70]

There are a number of supposedly haunted cemeteries throughout Ohio that contain the graves of people said to be witches. One bit of modern folklore concerns the Ridge Road Cemetery, also known as the Rehobeth Cemetery, in New Philadelphia. The second name was from the Rehobeth Church, which was in the vicinity until 1877. This is another haunted spot where dismembered body parts are said to move around on their own accord.

According to local belief, a man who practiced sorcery is buried here. One can indeed see his grave completely circled with a small stone wall. The tale goes that his head was cut off and buried in the same grave as the rest of his body, but it was placed at his feet. The head is said to be moving under the earth and will someday rejoin the body. Local lore assures us that anyone who lies down on the grave will die within a year. Local lore does not, however, explain why anyone would want to do that.[71]

In Richland, the Mount Olive Cemetery has the grave of a woman known as Bloody Mary, who was supposedly a witch. This is undoubtedly the woman known as Mary Jane Hendrickson, a Shawnee. Rather than a pointy-head villainess sending out legions of flying monkeys, this woman was an herbalist who used her skills with plants to cure people. If she had other powers or dark knowledge, one cannot be certain. Many who practiced herbal healing over the centuries have been accused of witchcraft.

Some local stories state that she was hanged as a witch or even burned at the stake. These are romantic tales, but the truth is not so fanciful. She died in 1898 at the young age of twenty-five. The cause of death was dropsy. There is a persistent legend that anyone who bothers or defaces her grave will die soon thereafter. According to the story, a girl who did this in 1952 soon died. Similarly, in 1985, a teenage couple defaced her grave, and they, too, soon died in an accident.

Another supposed witch who was said to be burned at the stake was the tragic Anna Mary Stockum, who is buried at (and is supposedly haunting) St. John's Lutheran Church Cemetery in Coshocton.

Mary and her husband, Christopher Stockum, had emigrated from Hessen, Germany. The couple had no less than nine children. When one was born severely handicapped, the father took the child out and murdered him. He was soon discovered, arrested and eventually hanged. The grieving widow apparently went mad. In revenge for losing her husband, she began to murder her other children. This also attracted the attention of the authorities, who supposedly put an end to her by burning her at the stake. But even after she was dead, the remaining children were becoming ill and seemed destined to follow their siblings to the grave.

The townspeople, in an act more common with vampirism than witchcraft, exhumed Mary's body and cut off her head. The head was buried outside of the consecrated ground of the graveyard, while the body remained inside of the perimeter of the hallowed ground of the cemetery. Both graves were covered by gravestones to keep the woman interred under the earth.

Apparently, the stones did not work. Her headless ghost has been seen many times wandering around the graveyard at night, searching for her lost head and shrieking out in the moonlight. Of course, there is also the more logical—although not nearly as dramatic—explanation of the two gravestones. Her original gravestone was replaced, and the old one was merely set aside by the fence.

Anyone wishing to search for her ghost should be forewarned that the area is adjacent to an abandoned strip mine. There are a number of deadly cliffs for the unwary, especially in the dark.[72]

The Elmwood Cemetery in Lancaster is so crowded with ghosts that one wonders how they don't bump into one another in the night. There is the spirit of a little girl seen running around the grounds as well as a menacing figure covered in a cloak and hood.

Unsurprisingly, this is also the location of one of Ohio's purported witch's graves.[73] In the Salem Church Cemetery in Wellston (we shall visit this graveyard in a later chapter) is supposedly the grave of yet another executed (that is, murdered) Ohio witch. People have felt her cool hand on their necks while walking through the grounds. There is little information about this sorceress, other than she was murdered and buried at the grounds before it became a cemetery.

If you need a job, you might want to apply to be a groundskeeper at the Salem Church Cemetery—it seems to have a rather difficult time keeping people on the payroll. After a short time, they often leave, complaining about icy hands grabbing them, whispering, shadows and even graves that change positions —not to mention the ghostly piano music that sometimes comes from the old empty church.

Before moving on to other topics, we must linger by the cauldron for a moment longer and turn our attention to that most deadly of witch curses: the dreaded feather crown.

FEATHER CROWNS

The belief that there is a power of evil working, which is ejaculated (as Bacon says) upon any object it beholds, has existed in all times and in all countries.[74]
—*Frederick Thomas Elworthy*

The first instance of feather crowns was at Riddle Street in Cincinnati in October 1875. Although once again the published account listed no names, in both instances, it was a German family who were seemingly the victims of a German witch.

It started innocently enough. A woman living in the Riddle Street area complained that she could not enjoy a decent night's sleep on her feather mattress, even though it was brand new. She had checked the feathers personally when she made the purchase and was certain that there were no chicken feathers but only soft down-like feathers from other birds. She then stuffed and sealed the mattress herself, thus no one could have interfered with it. However, she soon found that it was rough and uncomfortable—definitely not the way it was when it was first purchased.

Although it was utterly impossible, something had changed. Now, as she pulled out a blizzard of feathers, they were all from chickens. Curious about the reason for this, she opened the mattress a bit further to check the feathers. She found that there was something like a lump in it—something that had definitely not been there before.

Angrily, she pulled back the covering a bit more to find out what had caused the lump. She pulled the object out and nearly screamed. To her utter horror, she found a small doll-sized figure of a human baby made entirely of feathers.

Terrified, she gathered her German lady friends together, and as a group, they dared to open the rest of the mattress. As if it were a horror movie, they began to pull out hands, feet and legs and even small rats—all composed of feathers. These most certainly were not there when she had stuffed the mattress. Where could they have come from?

Of the neighbors who watched the dreadful scene, one made her living as a milliner—a woman who made hats. If anyone would know about working with feathers, it would be her. She took the objects and studied them closely. After a deep sigh, she shook her head and declared that she knew of no human hands that could have made such an object; they were far too intricate and perfect.

One of the elder German women watching this macabre unfolding finally spoke up. She begged the woman by all of her faith to take the devilish forms and consign them to the flames at once. She had seen such demonic things in the Old Country. These images, she explained, were the product of a *Hexe*, and if they were not burned, they would kill her. It did not take too much encouraging for the woman to follow suit on the request.

While this case was rather atypical, as it involved small figures, including a grotesque doll of a human baby, the item most often reported to form in a mattress is a circle of feathers. This is what is referred to as the dreaded feather crown.[75]

The old belief in the feather crown and the magical uses of feathers in pillows are not confined to the Germans. The concept is well known in the folklore of the South, particularly in the Appalachian region. However, we see something curious here. The opinion throughout Appalachia concerning the feather crown is divided and has two very different contradictory interpretations.

For many southerners who believe, there is no difference between their conclusion and that of the Germans in Ohio—the feather crown is the physical manifestation of a deadly curse placed by a witch with the intention of killing the person sleeping on the bed or the pillow. As with the Germans, they believe that the only way to end this curse is to take the feather crown and toss it into the fire, preferably while saying prayers.

However, there is also a completely opposite view. Some believe that if one of these is found in the bed or pillow of a person who has recently died, then it is a sure sign that the deceased has gone to heaven. Apparently, these feathers represent the wings of the angels carrying the soul to their reward in paradise. The angels would leave a token of the feathers from their wings in the shape of the crown of salvation that the person has earned by living a righteous life.[76] This interpretation is so prevalent that there are a number of people who have saved the crowns after they were discovered. There are some on display in museums in Appalachian regions and other parts of the South.

Similar to the German lore, voodoo practitioners believe that the pillow shapes will form very slowly, and when they have finished their construction, the victim will inevitably die. To make this even more macabre, the voodoo adherents state that, in the middle of the night, the victim may be troubled by the appearance of bird-like monsters in the pillow—all constructed from feathers. These unnatural creatures would form very slowly, night by night. During the time that they are coming together, the victim will become very ill and start to literally waste away. Only by removing and burning the supernatural effigies can the person be saved. If the little image is allowed to grow into completeness, the person will certainly die.

Voodoo practitioners who are impatient may take the express route and cut open a bird and place the wings in the pillow. Similar to this is the voodoo belief that putting bits of corn in the pillow will cause a child's growth to be stunted.

In the same year as the Riddle Street case, there was another incident involving witchcraft and curious things appearing in a mattress. This took place in one of the darkest parts of Cincinnati—that riverfront area known as Sausage and Rat Row, a vile district filled with saloons, brothels, cheap boardinghouses and every manner of sin. It would only stand to reason that witchcraft would be part of the dingy landscape.

We only know that the people involved were of Italian descent and had come to the country from Greece. For some undisclosed reason, there was bad blood between this family and an elderly woman. The source of the argument was not known.

The trouble came to a cauldron's boil when the father of the feuding group lost his temper, grabbed his gun and killed the old woman's cat. It was, of course, a black cat. Some might have speculated that it was the witch's familiar. Either way, killing the animal had disastrous consequences.

This did not sit well with the old woman who was supposedly a *strega*, the Italian word for "witch." According to a report at the time, "He was strong, but she was powerful, in mystical, unseen powers. She set her deadly spell on her enemy's child."[77] It is supposed that she fought back in her own way, casting a deadly curse on her attacker's family. This time, the target of the spell was an innocent little boy, just one year old, who was the son of the man who had shot the cat.

For some time, the child was ill and wasting away. The parents took him to physicians, but no one could help him. Finally, they decided that the only one who could help would be someone skilled in the dangerous practice of finding and stopping witches.

Located nearby on Vine Street was just such a man. Alexander Schilling was officially listed in the city directory as a fortuneteller. Apparently, he could do more than just read the future, as he had reportedly saved one little cursed boy who lived on Cross Street in the Mohawk district of Over-the-Rhine.

Schilling arrived at the home of the victims and looked at their sick child. Not happy with what he saw, he gave the family some strange powder to give to the child. But this was not the end of his examination, and things took a very decidedly bizarre turn. He had the boy removed to another room and told the parents that he then wanted them to tear apart the child's feather mattress. This made little sense, but who were they to argue with him?

They did so, only to find that growing in the bedding was a series of strangely colored feathers and, worst of all, the dreaded feather crown. This one was nearly completely formed—almost a full circle.

Cincinnati's Over-the-Rhine, where German immigrants brought belief in witchcraft to their new homeland. *From the collection of the Public Library of Cincinnati and Hamilton County.*

If anyone desired conclusive evidence of witchcraft, this was it. The *Cincinnati Enquirer* reported, "No one but a witch could have induced these things to grow on the inside of a feather bed which had not been re-stuffed or tampered with for twenty years. It was the work of a witch, and nothing short of a witch of the first water."[78]

The witch hunter was not at all surprised. He ordered the family to burn the offensive item at once. When this was done, he gave his prognosis. It was not what the family wanted to hear. He said that as a result of the fiery destruction of the crown, one of two people would invariably die. One of them might well be the witch. However, as things had gone unchecked for so long and the child had so badly wasted away, it might be the one-year-old boy. Either way, there was no escaping it—one would live, and the other would die.

Apparently, the curse had progressed too far. The child had suffered under the effects for far too long and was now beyond any hope of recovery. He died a short while later. The witch, however, lived on.

To some, it may be dismissed, stating that the poor boy was merely a victim of any of a number of deadly diseases that were endemic in that sordid district of Sausage and Rat Row. Others, however, would say that apparently the strega had her vengeance for the death of her beloved cat.

Another occurrence of witchcraft, feather crowns and curses came from Cleveland. As mentioned before, according to the modern occultist Dion Fortune, anyone who is subjected to a psychic attack, a more modern way to describe a curse, will have a number of things happen to them and their household. One of the most dangerous indications is the unexpected appearance of fires erupting spontaneously.

One such case, apparently the result of witchcraft, occurred in Cleveland in 1880. A German family, that of railroad worker John Busch and no less than eleven children, first lived on Lincoln Avenue. However, they quickly left the house, stating that it was haunted. Apparently, this was not the work of a traditional ghost, but something far more malevolent was being directed at them.

The family moved to a dwelling on Lusseenden Avenue. However, there were still disturbances, particularly the seemingly spontaneous eruption of fires. While it is tempting to state that with eleven children, one of them was probably a bit of a pyromaniac, the circumstances dispute this. In one case, the fire began in a closet that was sealed off by a bed. On another occasion, a pile of rags spontaneously erupted into flames. A hen had built its nest in a barrel in the yard and was either smoking in bed or the victim of the spell, for this, too, erupted in a blaze.

Word of these terrifying fires spread over the back fences throughout the neighborhood. Neighbors came to be with the family to try to protect them and to see for themselves what was going on. Despite the number of watchers, a fire spontaneously flared up in a mattress.

In the midst of all of this fear, an elderly German woman arrived and informed the family that they were undoubtedly under some kind of curse. To everyone's surprise, she stated emphatically that the only way to stop the horror was to open up the mattresses and search for a feather crown.

Although reluctant to tear up their bedding on her say, they were desperate. The family did as they were instructed. After tearing open the bedding, they saw to their amazement that the old woman was correct—there was indeed a feather crown forming in one of the mattresses. It was pulled out, and amid devout prayers, the offending item was boiled into nothingness.

Six years later, there was yet another case of feather crowns in Cincinnati. Once again, the chronicler did not give the names of the afflicted, only that this time the victim was a seven-year-old boy. He had previously been a normal, active child but suddenly fell deathly ill. He was literally wasting away, having been sick for nine weeks. He could not consume anything, save a little water.

One physician was summoned and tried a treatment, which had no effect. A more prominent doctor visited the child and stated that it was a case of that Victorian catch-all ailment brain fever. He also postulated that spinal meningitis may be the root of the problem. Of course, word of the child's illness was spoken from neighbor to neighbor over back fences. The German women of the neighborhood did not put the cause to meningitis but rather to *Hexerei*.

The *Enquirer* reporter gave the typical sarcastic critique of this diagnosis: "While the foibles of all people are to be respected, still the newspaper man was inclined to laugh when the story was told him of the way in which the work of imposing suffering on an innocent child had been accomplished by the knights of the broomstick."[79]

A committee of the German women visited the home and patiently explained to the grief-stricken mother that they believed witchcraft was the cause of her child's horrible illness. Shaking their heads, they stated in serious voices that they had seen such things before in the Old Country. They then asked permission to examine not the boy but his bed.

The mother had little patience or belief in the machinations of witches, but by now, she was desperate and willing to try anything to save her child. She readily consented. The group went into the dark room where the little boy remained suspended between life and death. The mother carefully picked him up and held him while the women silently went about the process of taking apart the feather mattress to see if anything evil was growing inside.

The mother was undoubtedly silently cursing herself for allowing a bunch of superstitious old biddies into her ill child's bedroom to rip up the bed. But then her doubt turned to horror. There, amid the mass of feathers that one would expect in a featherbed, were no less than five feather crowns.

The women patiently explained that it was witchcraft that was causing these items to form. Thankfully, the crowns had not yet joined at the ends, as they, like living unholy organisms, were still growing and forming. The women informed the mother that once the crowns came completely together it would be too late—the child would invariably die.

However, even though the wreaths were removed from the bed, the problem would not end. As long as these instruments of evil existed, the patient could not recover. The only possible cure was for the afflicted to take the wreaths, place a great deal of salt on them and consign them to flames. (According to some European beliefs, salt has the power to stop curses and even drive away evil spirits.) When the salted wreaths were burned to nothing, then the person could recover. If they were left in the bed, the ends would eventually join together and bring death. However, to allow them to continue to exist in a half-finished state was to place the person in a kind of horrible limbo, making the boy unable to either die or recover.

Then, as if things were not strange enough, the mother did something utterly inexplicable. Although she had evidence in her hands, she did not follow the sage advice of her friends. Rather than consigning them to the flames, the woman who previously did not believe in the supernatural took the feather crowns to "an old fortune-teller on Race Street, who is, so to speak, on good terms with the witches."[80]

This action made no logical sense. To cure her child, she had been informed that she would only need salt and a hearth, both of which she had. The women had even produced evidence of the bewitching. However, for some unknown logic, the mother of the sick child handed the deadly items over to a person who was seemingly aligned with the very people whose witchcraft had caused them to form in the first place.

The reporter completed the chronicle stating, "As it now stands the poor little fellow can neither get well nor die."[81]

A curious side note to this indicates that the innocent child may not have been the intended target of the curse. Twice the father of the house had taken the little mattress and used it as a pillow. However, when he did, he found that, for some unknown reason, he could not sleep and felt as though he were being choked. Apparently, the witchcraft would work on anyone who was reclining on the mattress.

The mention of the unnamed fortuneteller on Race Street brings to mind a bizarre case from two years after this occurrence, involving a German woman living on Race Street. This was Mrs. Josephina Lindecker, the widow of a Mr. John Lindecker. Although her actual profession was listed as dealing in hair care products, she was well known in the neighborhood as a fortuneteller, having specialized in herbs and other folk remedies. In this wild incident, she was accused of using witchcraft against a local family.

The case in which this particular fortuneteller from Race Street was involved is a very strange one dating to the horrific occurrences on March 26, 1883, in the heavily German neighborhood of Over-the-Rhine. Some skeptics may believe that it was merely the case of a superstitious family going a bit crazy. To occultists, it bears the unmistakable markings of either a poltergeist or a genuine occurrence of psychic attack.

A little before midnight, Michael Scheffler, followed by his entire family, ran into the Bremen Street (since the First World War, the street has been known as Republic Street) police station in a state of pure panic. The

Race St., north from 13th, Cincinnati.

Over-the-Rhine, showing Race Street when Josephina Lindecker lived in the neighborhood. *From the collection of the Public Library of Cincinnati and Hamilton County.*

parade of terrified people included not only Michael but also his wife, a young man and woman and two smaller boys. After catching his breath, the panic-stricken Mr. Scheffler related to the desk sergeant a bizarre tale of witchcraft and horror.

The flabbergasted sergeant turned the matter over to Lieutenant Westendorf, who, no doubt giving the sergeant an angry glance or two, listened as patiently as he could to the people's story.

First, they declared that they had been suffering for some time, but the haunting had become so violent that they refused to spend another night in their apartment. Could the lieutenant help them? Was there someplace that they could find shelter?

Yes, they could go into the cell room and rest there. This calmed them a bit, allowing the policeman to gather information.

The family lived nearby in an apartment at 180 Liberty Street between Bremen and Race. The officer knew the building well. It was owned by a Mr. George Meyers, a respectable man. There were nearly a dozen families residing in the structure.

The Schefflers, in excited voices, related a bizarre tale of haunting and witchcraft. They had lived in the apartment for nine months. The first seven of these were completely without incident. Then, for the last two, they were under constant supernatural attack. That is when they had begun to deal with the witch. Witch? What witch?

For those two months, they had, as they claimed, suffered the evil spells cast by a local old German woman, a fortuneteller who lived right on the southeast corner of Race and Liberty Streets at 572 Race Street. Her name was Mrs. Jospehina Lindecker. The disturbances only happened after they had become involved with her.

Still quite agitated, Scheffler related a strange tale to the police and a few newspaper reporters who just happened to be passing the time in the station waiting to see if something would come up. (Boy, did they ever have their wish granted.) One of those listening in was a reporter for the *Cincinnati Commercial Gazette* and another was from the *Cincinnati Enquirer*.

Scheffler said that he refused to take another step in the house because it was besieged by evil spirits brought on by the *Hexe*. The attacks had come for some time and had been getting progressively worse. The phenomenon, as happens in many poltergeist cases, began with strange rapping sounds. As this became more pervasive over the following days, members of the family began to see what is now often referred to as shadow people—dark ghostlike humanoid figures flitting around the apartment.

The building that Josephina Lindecker lived in still stands today. The scaffolding on the church shows the revitalization of this historic neighborhood. *Photo Douglas R. Weise.*

From here, the encounters became physical. Members of the family would sometimes feel themselves being patted by invisible hands. Later, this became more aggressive, including being pinched and scratched.

Mr. and Mrs. Scheffler were in their bed one night when, for no reason, both of them were suddenly tossed out of the bed and onto the floor. The eldest boy, Fred, saw this happen. He stated that just before it happened, one of those shadowy things, looking like what he described as a gigantic rat, had rushed out of the nearby wardrobe and attacked the bed.

Once, when Mrs. Scheffler was putting some coal into the stove, an unseen hand pushed her to the floor. Another time, something unseen actually picked her up and tried to put her into the stove. She "was just in the act of touching a match to the kindling when some invisible agent seized her by the back of the neck and…her dress and almost stood the estimable woman on her head in the place where the stove-lid should go."[82] Not surprisingly, the "estimable woman" fainted and had to be taken out into the yard and revived.

The young boy went to bed one night, but to his horror, something unseen grabbed his feet and pulled him. This was not the first time that he was a victim of a spectral attack, for he had already suffered having pins thrust into him.

When Michael lay down to sleep, he suffered freezing chills, a kind of paralysis and a weight on his chest, what the old Germans sometimes referred to as an attack by the nightmare demon known as the alp. (The German word for nightmare is *Alptraum*.) Mrs. Scheffler stated that as a remedy against witchcraft, she had consecrated some paper flowers and then burned them in the stove. The spell apparently did not work.

Finally, the family could stand it no longer and fled their haunted residence, seeking assistance from civil authorities.

The lieutenant was astounded and a bit confused. This was an exciting tale, certainly something to share with his wife when he came home, but what could he do? It was not against the law to be haunted. It was not even against the law to be a ghost. He would have a heck of a time handcuffing a spirit.

But as the terrified Scheffler family obviously was not going anywhere until this matter was settled, he figured that he should send someone to investigate. Sergeant Austin was the lucky man chosen for the job. The only one of the Scheffler family brave enough to reenter the apartment was the eldest son, Fred. However, the small company of curious reporters was not about to miss this opportunity. They grabbed their coats and their notebooks and followed the policeman and the boy like a small parade.

Once everyone entered the apartment, some banging and shuffling was immediately heard. The sergeant swung his lantern around just as something small ran toward them. Perhaps the spooky occasion was working on him, for his first reaction was to hit it with his club. There was, instead of a groaning ghost, a sharp yelp of pain. He shined the lantern down to reveal that the assailant was a mortal and rather common puppy. However, the young Scheffler, in a frightened tone, declared that it was the spirit. The boy had no idea where the puppy had come from. He had never seen it before.

After everyone caught their breath, the search of the apartment resumed. Rather like a modern automobile that refuses to malfunction in front of a mechanic, absolutely nothing particularly supernatural occurred in their presence. No one in the group was knocked over, no one saw shadowy figures flitting about and no one was picked up by their pants and shoved into the oven. It was now time for the group to proceed on to the next phase of this investigation.

The group walked around the corner of Liberty and Race to confront the witch herself. They found her sitting in a rocking chair calmly knitting and a bit surprised at her late-night visitors. She was described with "an ordinary shawl over her head, and not as had been expected, brewing deadly concoctions in magic cauldrons, while grim and grisly emblems of her calling were ranged about. She didn't look like one of the witches in 'Macbeth' nor like a hag. She resembled the usual old German woman in every particular of form and features and attire."[83]

Besides her hair care business, Mrs. Jospehina Lindecker (sarcastically referred to as Frau Lindecker in the *Gazette* and Madame in the *Enquirer*) made a meager living telling fortunes and selling small herbal remedies to her neighbors.

Sergeant Austin was at a loss, for there is no Ohio law against witchcraft. However, there is a law against distributing medicine without a medical license. On this rather trumped-up charge, he now had the excuse to escort her back to the station, where she could face her accusers. Most of the accusers, however, did not want to face the suspected witch, at least not eye to eye. They directed their gaze at the floor, apparently fearful of the evil eye.

It was here that the old widow revealed herself to be rather crafty. She freely admitted that she did indeed give Mr. Scheffler some peppermint tea, as he had some bowel trouble. There is certainly no law against giving a man a cup of tea. As to her selling and distributing medicine, she emphatically denied the charge. Nothing was actually *sold*, as she informed the officers at the station. Everything she did was for free; however, if the grateful recipient wanted to give her a reward in return for her helpful herbal remedies, who was she to refuse?

Now things were becoming very interesting. There was a great discrepancy between the amount of money involved. Mrs. Lindecker claimed that she had only received five dollars as a gift for helping Mr. Scheffler with his stomach ailment. (Keep in mind that in 1883, five dollars was of much greater value than it is today.) The Scheffler family, however, claimed that they had paid her twenty-two dollars over a period of time. Could this disagreement over money be the motive for someone to cast a spell on a family? That would be for the legal system to decide.

Mrs. Lindecker was bound over to police court to face charges of unlicensed medical activity. It was determined that "she [Mrs. Lindecker] is undoubtedly the cause of the present trouble, as by her threats and peculiar medical treatment she seems to have infected the entire family with their mild crankiness or lunacy."[84]

The *Gazette* ended its discussion of the Schefflers' "mild crankiness or lunacy" with an assessment of Michael Scheffler: "Mr. Scheffler in particular, appears to be considerably more than half crazy, and is in mortal terror at even the sight of the old woman."[85]

The wife moved in with some neighbors until the matter could be resolved. However, the next day, when Mr. Scheffler and his sons returned to the apartment in daylight to retrieve some items, he excitedly stated that he was being scratched by what he thought was an invisible cat. After this, he remained living at the police station, where he made a complete nuisance of himself to his uniformed hosts. "He raved about specters, witches and charms like a madman, and it is believed by the officers in charge of the station that he really is insane."[86]

The legal case against Josephina Lindecker came to naught. Taken to police court the next day, she was granted a continuance. When she faced the judge on April 4, he wanted no part of the Halloween fantasy. The entire charge was dismissed.

It is interesting to note that no one checked the feather mattresses, though that appeared to be the usual procedure among the Germans when one believed that they were under a curse. Instead, the newspapers shared a good laugh and inevitably blamed the victim.

Sadly, there is no way of knowing if the fortuneteller living on Race Street in the first account is the same Mrs. Lindecker who lived on the same street. One must wonder just how many fortunetellers lived on Race Street in Over-the-Rhine?

Was Mr. Scheffler "more than half crazy?" If so, then his entire family had to be a bit looney. Was Mrs. Lindecker just a harmless old woman who read palms and tea leaves and sold herbs to sick people, or was she, perhaps, Cincinnati's most famous witch, dwelling at the busy intersection of Liberty and Race Streets?

GHOSTS OF THINGS THAT SHOULD NOT BE GHOSTS

A most ghastly place; its leprous walls and deadly moisture;
its stones seem to sweat an icy and deathlike dampness; the vaulted roof
and sides are covered with growths of white fungi, hideous and poisonous,
ghastly exhalations seem to rise from its floor.
—Cincinnati Commercial, *August 29, 1875*

Turning now from witches to ghosts, we must first note that the Buckeye State has a long list of hauntings—far too many to catalogue here. The Ohio Penitentiary is a veritable cauldron of supernatural activity, as are many other prisons, hospitals and insane asylums. Like other states, Ohio has no shortage of women in white, such as the one in the Old Baptist Cemetery in Jackson, the younger girl in the Old Logan Cemetery in Logan, the one often seen crossing the Lucy Run Cemetery Road in Batavia or the lady haunting the Ye Olde Tavern in Yellow Springs (this one wears blue). Ohio has plenty of ghost children, such as the one in the Veterans Memorial Hospital in Pomeroy, the Amber Rose Restaurant in Dayton, the building housing the Fulton County Historical Society in Wauseon or the one who cries on the Ghormley Road Bridge in Greenfield. Ohio certainly has more than its share of haunted theaters, such as the Twin City Opera House in McConnelsville, the old Valentine Theatre in Defiance and the Schines Strand Theatre in Delaware, to say nothing of the man in a yellow raincoat haunting the Agora Theatre in Cleveland.

However, as there are so many, we will limit ourselves to the more unusual hauntings, especially those with really good stories behind them.

In this chapter, we will take a quick look at some ghosts that should not be ghosts, seeing as they were never alive—or never human—in the first place.

First among these is what may well be Ohio's most famous phantom, even if it was just passing through. On April 29 of each year, hundreds of people line the railroad tracks in Urbana waiting for the arrival of the ghost of the funeral train of the fallen president Abraham Lincoln.

At the end of the Civil War, the sixteenth president had a terrible dream that he related to his wife and a few close friends. He dreamed that he was walking through the White House late at night when he came upon a coffin with a soldier standing honor guard. Asking who had passed, he was informed that the president had been assassinated.

Lincoln's premonitions continued. On Good Friday, April 14, he stated that he did not want to attend the play *Our American Cousin* at Ford's Theatre. In fact, he had already seen the play but felt that a sense of destiny compelled him to be there.

In the section of the play when a comic rustic character delivers a humorous soliloquy, actor and Confederate sympathizer John Wilkes Booth crept into the presidential box. He knew that everyone's attention would be

A vintage shot of Urbana, a typical small town. Not so typical is that a president's ghost rolls through each year. *Library of Congress.*

Major Henry Rathbone (*standing*) was haunted by guilt. In 1883, he shot his wife and then stabbed himself, reenacting the assassination he couldn't stop. *Library of Congress.*

on the funny character on the stage and that there would be the sound of laughter. Booth shot Lincoln in the back of the head and then wrestled with the other guest, army major Henry Rathbone. After stabbing the major, he leaped from the box onto the stage and, with a broken leg, managed to make his escape before a shocked audience.

Lincoln was carried across the street to a small rooming house, where he died.

Secretary of War Edwin M. Stanton took over arrangements for the funeral. It was determined that a special train would be enlisted to carry not only the body of Abraham Lincoln but also the remains of his son Willie, who had died from typhoid while Lincoln was president. Father and son were making the final journey to their home state.

The funeral train followed the same route that Lincoln traveled when he left Illinois for Washington, D.C., although the cities of Cincinnati and Pittsburgh were excluded. The train was routed farther north, taking it right through the small town of Urbana. The tracks were lined with mourners as the funeral train made its way through the 1,654-mile route. No matter what time the train passed through the big cities or small towns, people were lined up along the tracks, many weeping as the fallen president passed. It finally arrived in Springfield, Illinois, on May 3.

Lincoln's funeral train, whose ghost would go through Urbana and other cities right on schedule, stopping clocks in its wake. *Library of Congress.*

Parts of that gloomy journey have been repeated in ghostly form year after year. The ghost train seen by hundreds of witnesses over the decades is not like the actual train seen by the living mourners in 1865. The cars on this phantom train are open, revealing a large company of skeletons dressed in blue uniforms. The spectral train makes its way in complete silence. However, should a physical locomotive from this world pass by at the same time, its sound is silenced as well, as if demanding respect for the fallen president.

One curious phenomenon has been reported countless times over the years. In the area near the passing of the ghost train, all watches and clocks suddenly stop—even if the inhabitants of the house are not paying the slightest attention to the ghostly events taking place outside.

For many years in Urbana, it was an annual event to stand by the tracks on Miami Street and wait for the ghost train. Many people saw it, and many people had to reset their watches and clocks. However, as the years pass by, there have been fewer and fewer sightings of the phantom train, as though it, too, is fading away.[87]

Some of the most bizarre Ohio hauntings involve not just the spirits of people but also the appearance of buildings or other places that no longer exist. It is as though an uncanny portal to the past suddenly opens.

One of these is the occasional sighting of a War of 1812 fort in Lima. Known as Fort Amanda, the garrison was used as a supply base during the war. The sudden manifestation of a log cabin is seen most often immediately after a thunderstorm. Should a person walk toward it, the structure will simply vanish. In the nearby cemetery, strange whispering voices are sometimes heard and ghostly lights zip about.[88]

A phantom house has also been reported as appearing in Old Egypt Cemetery near Flushing. Just like Fort Amanda, if one approaches this house, it will disappear. This is only one of a number of reported haunts in and around the cemetery.

Even more bizarre than a phantom fort or house is the supernatural appearance of an entire amusement park. In 1903, Jackson County coal baron C.K. Davis purchased land in Lake Alma to construct an amusement park. It was quite popular and featured rides and a dance hall. However, in 1910, the nearby city of Wellston decided that it needed the area for a water supply. To serve the greater public good, the park was closed. However, apparently, some people did not want to give up their day at the pleasure ground. Every so often, people see the ghost of the amusement park with people having the time of their afterlives.[89]

Ghostly dancers have also been seen tripping the light fantastic in Cincinnati's Coney Island at the old Moonlight Gardens. However, no music can be heard.

While we're on the subject of amusement parks, how about a haunted carousel? Cedar Point itself is not a ghost. It has been around since 1870 and is still going strong as Ohio's most famous amusement park. However, the ornate carousel in Frontiertown used to have one very haunted steed—the world's only haunted carousel animal, with quite a story behind it.

The horse, known as the military horse, was carved by Daniel C. Muller around 1917. What Muller did not know was that his wife was fooling around with a local jockey. When he found out, he murdered her and her illicit lover. Some versions of the story state that he stuffed her body into the horse, while others say that the cuckolded husband carved representations of their bones on the mechanical steed. A more sedate version of the tale affirms that she was a faithful wife but for some reason loved this one particular horse that her husband had carved.

Either way, she began to ride the horse after her death. It has been reported that the carousel would sometimes start up on its own power at night after the park had closed. Those who came to investigate the lights and calliope music would be astonished to see a woman in white riding her favorite horse. Other times, the various horses and other animals would be found in the morning in wrong positions—all except for the military horse. Sometimes, people who attempted to get on that animal would be shoved off by an unseen force.

One can still see the military horse but not on the famous carousel. The amusement park management decided that enough was enough. The horse is now on display in the park but no longer carries children. If you visit the horse, listen carefully. Some say that you can sometimes hear Mrs. Muller walking around near her beloved horse.[90]

Chester Park in Cincinnati closed its doors in 1932. The grounds later become the offices of a far less carefree institution—the Cincinnati Water Works. However, some people are still having a good time there. Besides things moving around on their own and strange sounds, one can occasionally hear the bouncing of a ball, still playing a game that should have ended about a century earlier.

Another Ohio amusement park with more traditional ghosts is found in Warren County at Kings Island. Although it is not accessible by patrons, there is a pioneer-era cemetery on the grounds known as the Dog Street Cemetery. Workers and visitors, especially those riding the train, sometimes see a little girl in a blue dress running along having a great time. This is presumed to be the ghost of five-year-old Missouri Jane Galeenor, who left this world in 1846 and was buried in the little graveyard. Who can blame her for wanting to have a day at an amusement park?

Kings Island also features a one-third-size replica of the Eiffel Tower. This spot is also supposedly haunted by the spirit of a young man who fell to his death from the structure.[91]

Moving on from the happy world of amusement parks, one hardly knows what to make of the mysterious case of a phantom artist from Cincinnati's East End. Today, the area of the East End once known as Fulton, due to the steamboat construction in the area, is being revitalized with expensive condominiums purchased at top dollar by young professionals wanting to live with a view of Old Man River. However, in 1896, this was an area that was often overlooked, with poor families who made their living on the river and put up with being forced out of their homes every few years by floods.

One of the features of the area was Carter Street, which no longer exists. Nearby was a forgotten cemetery—one that went back to the founding of the city a little more than a century earlier. Living right next to the graveyard was a widow, Mary J. Karnes.

Kings Island amusement park is supposedly haunted by two ghosts, but these are merely Halloween decorations. *Library of Congress.*

Kings Island's showpiece is this replica of the Eiffel Tower, supposedly haunted by the ghost of a teenager. *Library of Congress.*

However, some power from that unused resting place did not want to be forgotten. Something was sending messages to the world of the living, and it used a very bizarre method. When Mrs. Karnes entered her house, she would invariably find something etched on one of her pieces of glass—windows, lamp globes, whatever. One time, on the chimney of one of her oil lamps, there was the unmistakable impression of the letter *A*.

It was not only letters; sometimes pictures would appear as well. Once, it was a woman holding a rope, possibly the depiction of someone about to commit suicide. Another time, there was an entire steamboat etched, showing it stranded on an iceberg. (While this may seem a bit fantastic, sometimes the Ohio River would freeze in bitterly cold winters, posing a grave danger to inland water traffic. In 1918, the Coney Island steamboat *Princess* was crushed in just such a situation.) As amazing as these cynosures were, they would not last. Although they were etched right on the glass, within two hours, they had vanished as mysteriously as they appeared.

All of Mrs. Karnes's neighbors and many others came to her small cottage to look at these curiosities, hoping to solve the mystery. No one could find a rational explanation. All left shaking their heads, perhaps making a sign of the cross and without a doubt taking a furtive glance at the old overgrown cemetery right next to her cottage.[92]

While there has always been debate as to whether or not animals have souls, there is no argument that Ohio has a number of prominent animal ghosts. One of the most peculiar is in Athens County.

Usually, when the ghost of an animal is seen, it is connected to a human being. However, the ghost seen in Strouds Run State Park in Athens County is quite different. It is the ghost of what is believed to be the very last buffalo to be hunted in the state of Ohio. As it was the last, a local law stated that it could not be hunted. A soldier from either the French or British army (there is disagreement over which one) disobeyed the order and killed the beast. The ghost is sometimes seen at a stream drinking.

This is not the only specter seen in the area. R.J. Abraham not once but twice encountered the ghost of an Indian he believed to be Tecumseh. Apparently, there were no ill feelings on the part of the spirit, as on one occasion, Abraham was headed toward a collision after a brake failure, when an Indian suddenly appeared in the car with him and turned the wheel away from the potential accident.[93]

If Tecumseh and a ghost buffalo aren't enough, there is the bizarre tale of a ghost steer appearing on the country road near Lancaster. It is quite a tale.

The story behind the ghostly bovine involves a strange case of murder in the early nineteenth century. It took place on a country dirt road known as Foglesong Road. It involved the murder of a man named John Ornsdorff, supposedly by a moonshiner known as Old Man Crowley.

Ornsdorff was riding along Foglesong Road one night when something happened to him. He never returned home, but his horse did, without a rider, blood smeared on the saddlebags. A group of men went out searching for answers. They found the spot where the struggle had taken place and a bloody trail indicating where a body had been dragged. The trail led them right to Old Man Crowley's place.

The door to his barn and still was locked, but with axes and timbers, they broke it down. On entering, the posse found the source of the trail and the blood: a freshly killed steer. There was no sign of Old Man Crowley or John Ornsdorff.

Soon after that, Foglesong Road was said to be haunted. One night, Jacob Spangler rode down the road, albeit quite reluctantly. He had no choice, as he was going in search of a doctor to aid an ill family member. Suddenly, the road was blocked—not by the ghost of either human but rather the shade of a steer. As he tried to divert the horse, the steer actually climbed up on the steed. Jacob had no choice but to ride along with the ghost cow. As soon as he passed the spot where the murder supposedly took place, the steer vanished.

Spangler was not the only person to have witnessed the phantom bovine. There are those who to this day claim to see or hear the ghost of old Foglesong Road, now known as Stringtown Road. This old area of Still-House Hollow was located near what is now Keller-Kirn Park.[94]

Near Glouster is the famous Tinker's Cave, named after the notorious horse thief Shepard Tinker. The story goes that in the mid-nineteenth century, Tinker was not originally a horse thief but an obnoxious loudmouth who liked to drink too much. One night while sitting in the tavern bragging about made-up accomplishments, he declared that he had stolen a neighbor's horse and rode it around the county.

Of course, no one believed this teller of tall tales—no one except the man who owned the horse. He demanded that the law arrest the man who had illegally borrowed his horse. With this, Shep Tinker decided that if he was going to be accused of a crime, he might as well commit the crime. As his employment opportunities were not particularly good at the moment, he decided to engage in horse thievery full time.

He soon became quite well known as a horse thief. It was rumored that he even supplied fresh horses to General John Morgan's Confederate raiders, which would make him both a thief and a traitor. It is, no doubt, for this reason that immediately after the Civil War, Shep decided on a change of address to a place where people did not know him or his exploits during the war. The cave where he corralled his stolen steeds is known as Tinker's Cave. It is said that people can still hear the neighing of the horses.[95]

Another spot in Ohio where one can hear ghost horses is at Scotts Creek Falls near Logan. In 1887, a young newly married couple, Clara and Johannes Bensenhafer, were crossing Scott's Creek, when the wagon suddenly fell into the underwater hole aptly named the Death Hole. Due to a strong undertow, neither of the humans nor the horses could escape. To this day, one can sometimes hear their casual conversation and then their screams, including the cries of the horses, as they plunge to their deaths in the water.[96]

In the Otterbein United Methodist Church Cemetery on Country Road 62, near Northwest Rushville, amid the old monuments is the grave of Mary Henry, now forever marked with the blood-red imprint of a horse's hoof, and there is quite a story behind it.

The year was 1844. Mary's soon-to-be-husband, James Kennedy Henry, had the unique problem of having two pretty young girls who wanted to marry him. One was Mary Angle, and the other was Rachael Hodge. He could not decide which would be his bride. As the story goes, probably with more than a bit of romantic embellishment, he fell asleep riding his horse one night and woke up in front of Mary's house. Obviously, this was a sure sign that Providence wanted him to marry Mary. The two were soon wed, and the spurned Rachael was not the bride but a bridesmaid.

Both sets of in-laws gave the new couple a horse so they could start their own farm. The happiness did not last long, as a year later, Mary, like so many women at the time, died during childbirth. Tradition compelled James to return the wedding gift of the horse. He did not. Three years later, after a proper period of mourning, he went with plan B and married Rachael.

Mary's parents were having financial troubles and really needed the horse they had given. It was not intended for this young man and another woman. However, there was no offer forthcoming to return the steed. As it had been a gift, they could hardly ask for it.

Rachael, understanding the precarious position she was in, encouraged her new husband to not forget his first wife. On their wedding day in December, she wore mourning black rather than the virginal white dress. After the ceremony, the two went to Mary's grave to leave some offerings and say a prayer for her. Apparently, Mary was not in the least bit happy

The gravestone of Mary Henry has been broken but is now braced together. A small fence protects it against vandalism *Photo by Douglas R. Weise.*

about the new arrangement. A frigid gale-force wind came from nowhere and blew the newlyweds away from her grave.

It was about this time that the mysterious bloody imprint of the horseshoe was found on Mary's grave. A decade went by, during which time James and Rachael had four children. But the anger from beyond would not be quenched. One April night in 1859, the sexton at the Otterbein Cemetery saw a blazing fireball above Mary's grave. Suddenly, it flew up into the air and exploded in a dazzling light as though it were the Fourth of July. Before he could react to this, he heard the sound of a galloping horse headed straight toward the Henry farm. He just turned and walked away. He knew that before long he would have some work to do.

The very next day, James was in the barn. The normally docile horse that Mary's parents had given him—and he refused to return—suddenly kicked him in the head, snapping his neck. It was a horse that brought him to Mary, it was a horse that he had received as a wedding present, it was a horse's hoof that was imprinted on her grave, it was the sound of a horse that presaged his death and it was a horse that killed him.

The imprint of the hoof is still there for anyone who wants to see it. The grave has since been put in metal casing, as it is disintegrating, and a small fence is around it to protect it from vandals. There has been more than one person who has also reported seeing a bluish light floating above the grave or hearing the sound of a galloping horse in the cemetery.[97]

There are a number of cases of cat ghosts in Ohio. Perhaps the most famous is the story of the Calico Lady in Ripley, Ohio. Ripley, famous for the Rankin House, was one of the most active stops along the Underground Railroad. Hundreds of escaped slaves passed through the house and the city on their way to freedom in Canada.

Another old house can be seen at the end of Lafferty Road and Chicken Hollow. However, anyone wishing to investigate must do so on foot, as the bridge is out. This is the area haunted by the infamous Calico Lady.

When James Henry died from being kicked by a horse, this inexplicable horseshoe image appeared on Mary's gravestone. *Photo by Douglas R. Weise.*

Left: Close-up view of the mysterious horseshoe mark. The ghostly sound of a horse is sometimes heard in this rural churchyard. *Photo by Douglas R. Weise.*

Below: The Rankin House in Ripley along the Ohio River. This was a major station in the Underground Railroad. *Library of Congress.*

The story is a sad one. Her patriotic husband joined the army when the Civil War broke out. Each day, the woman would walk to the corner of the road to wait for mail or news about her husband. But no letter was coming because he had died in the terrible conflict.

Despite the fact that her husband was now dead, the woman continued her ritual, only now she would go to the same spot and weep. For this reason, she is also known as the Weeping Widow. Like many other ghosts, it is said that if you call out her name three times at night, she will materialize and chase you. It is also stated that should you accidentally run into the specter, you must promptly return with a bunch of flowers, as one would place on a grave. Failure to do so would be considered most dangerous and might cost your life.

One young man had the misfortune of seeing the Weeping Widow and inquired of his grandfather what he should do. The old man knew about the ghost and told him to return with some flowers as an offering. The young man returned to apologize but did not want to spend money on flowers. A few weeks later, he was drafted and soon died in combat, just as the Calico Lady's husband did.

Although the Weeping Widow shunned the company of people for the rest of her life, she did enjoy having a lot of cats. Thus if she materializes at the crossroads, one may very well expect to be chased by yowling cats. There is some debate as to whether the Calico Lady and the Weeping Widow are the same woman.

Ripley seems to have an attraction to ghost cats. The Baird Bed and Breakfast is haunted by a phantom feline, as well as an opera singer. Florence Baird was an accomplished singer and even sang with the Metropolitan Opera. Her ghostly voice can still be heard at the bed-and-breakfast, but sadly, she is only warming up by practicing scales. If one wants to hear an otherworldly aria from *Tannhäuser*, sadly this is not the place.[98]

Undoubtedly, the best-known cat ghost in Ohio is in the north part of the state bordering Lake Erie. Here, one may visit the Fairport Harbor Lighthouse and possibly feel the soft fur of a cat rub against your leg. However, you will not see the feline.

The lighthouse was built in 1825 and was first operated by Samuel Butler. Besides watching over ships in Lake Erie, Butler looked after his fellow man. This lighthouse was a way station—one of the very last in the Underground Railroad. Many men and women, fleeing from bondage in the South, hid in the cellar of the old building. Once it was safe, the slaves were smuggled across Lake Erie to Canada. When they had moved north of the border, they were free.

The lighthouse was refurbished in 1871, when Captain Joseph Babcock and his wife became the keepers. His wife grew ill but was helped through her sickness by the presence of a large number of cats. The living quarters where Mrs. Babcock enjoyed the feline company is now a museum. People visiting and working in the museum reported feeling or sometimes seeing a solitary ghost cat. But why should there be only one cat when she apparently had many?

The answer may have been discovered when the building was renovated and a new air conditioning system installed. One of the workmen digging in the walls made a gruesome discovery. There was a mummified cat. Mrs. Babcock owned many cats, but there was only one entombed in the wall. Could this have been her favorite?[99]

Perhaps she had nothing to do with it—the animal may have been a sacrifice in what is known as a builder's rite. For centuries, particularly in the low countries of northern Europe, human beings, later substituted with animals, were entombed in the foundations of new buildings to prevent the structures from collapsing. It was then believed that the spirit of the sacrifice would remain on-site to protect the structure.

Paul Carus mentions this in his classic work *The History of the Devil and the Idea of Evil*:

> *In Tommaseo's Canti Populari an instance is quoted of the voice of an archangel from heaven bidding the builders of a wall entomb the wife of the architect in its foundation. The practice is here regarded as Christian and it is apparent that there are instances in which Christian authorities were sufficiently ignorant to sanction it, for even the erection of churches was supposed to require the same cruel sacrifice; and there were cases in which, according to the special sanctity of the place, it was deemed necessary to bury a priest, because children or women were not regarded as sufficient. In Günther's Sagenbuch des Deutschen Volkes (Vol. I., p. 33 ff.) we read that the Strassburg cathedral required the sacrifice of two human lives, and that two brothers lie buried in its foundation.* [100]

When you visit the Fairport Lighthouse Museum, you might also keep an eye out for a five-year-old boy running up and down the stairs. His name is Robbie, and he died many years ago of smallpox.

A ghost dog can be found in the Center of Science and Industry in Columbus. Many workers and volunteers have felt the dog rub against them.

The Woodland Cemetery near the University of Dayton is one of the most beautiful memorial gardens in the state, and a number of famous people are buried there, including the Wright Brothers and the marvelous comic writer Erma Bombeck. It also has a sad ghost. According to the tale, in 1860, a five-year-old boy named Johnny Morehouse fell and drowned in the Miami Erie Canal. His dog stood watch over his grave and refused to leave. Now, the two can sometimes be seen at night running and having a good time together at last. His grave features the statue of a boy and a

Daniel La Dow's moving statue marking Johnny Morehouse's grave. The ghosts of both have been seen playing in the cemetery. *Photo Douglas R. Weise.*

dog, carved by Daniel La Dow. Many people leave coins or little trinkets as offerings—and a few dog biscuits as well.

The same cemetery houses the story of a woman who likes to go up to people and have a bit of a conversation. Then she vanishes. There is also a glowing grave and many reports of people seeing a girl in blue jeans weeping over a grave and then disappearing.[101]

Now we must leave the peaceful world of ghost horses, cows, buffalo, cats and dogs and turn our attention to the grislier domain of cataclysm and homicide.

GRUESOME AND GHOSTLY

DISASTERS AND MURDER MOST FOUL

There are six things the Lord hates, seven that are detestable to him:
haughty eyes, a lying tongue, hands that shed innocent blood.
—Proverbs 6:16–17

Hauntings often occur at the sites of disasters or terrible bloodshed. This makes sense, for this is where lives are cut short in an instant. Places marred by unexpected disasters, natural or man-made; battlefields; murders scenes—these are where the spirits of some victims sometimes linger in this world, as though confused or overwhelmed by the bloody turn of events.

One of the most famous Ohio haunted calamity spots is the site of the dreadful Ashtabula train wreck. It was the night of December 29, 1876. In the midst of a blizzard, the Lake Shore and Michigan Southern Railway Pacific Express Number 5 was steaming toward the Ashtabula Bridge. The stress of the weight of the train and the frigid temperatures caused a structural failure. In an instant, the passenger cars fell seventy feet to the icy waters of the Ashtabula River below.

As soon as the cars hit the ice, a number of oil lamps shattered, spraying oil throughout the cars and igniting them. Those who were not killed in the crash either died or were seriously injured from the fires.

In the end, ninety-eight people died in the crash, and sixty-four had serious injuries. To make matters even more mysterious, there has been a persistent rumor that the train was quietly carrying a shipment of gold bullion worth $2 million. If it is true, no one has uncovered the treasure yet.

Nineteen of the dead, many of them burned beyond recognition, were taken to the Chestnut Grove Cemetery. In 1895, a granite marker was erected to honor the dead, both known and unknown, from that disaster.

There are numerous hauntings at both the site of the wreck and at the cemetery. People have seen small lights floating around. Others have seen ghostly figures wandering as though lost. Some have heard screams of terror, while some people have reported a burning smell.

There is another ghost haunting the Chestnut Grove Cemetery. It is that of Charles Collins, the safety inspector who did not see the stress of the metal in the bridge and proclaimed that it was safe. Ironically, he was buried in the same graveyard as the victims. His ghost is sometimes seen sitting near his ornate mausoleum weeping and begging for forgiveness.[102]

This is not the only site in Ohio that is haunted by the victims of a train wreck. On Maud Hughes Road in Liberty Township, Butler County, there is the infamous Screaming Bridge. Sometimes people driving over the bridge hear screams. The cause of this was a train accident in 1909 in which two railroad men lost their lives, reportedly from being scalded to death by an exploding boiler. The steam engine was filled with water when it left Ivorydale, but no one noticed that it was leaking. Three other people were injured in the blast.[103]

Another area haunted by the victims of railroad disasters is the Blue Limestone Park in Delaware County north of Columbus. Balls of light are sometimes seen floating around. A brick tunnel beneath the railroad tracks is also haunted by whispering voices.[104]

Another famous haunted disaster site is at Millfield in Athens County. The Millfield Mine Disaster occurred on November 5, 1930. Poston Mine Number 6, was said to be the safest in the company and in the entire Hocking Valley region. However, at 11:45 a.m. in the 6 section, an electrical arc between the iron rail and a fallen trolley wire suddenly ignited the gas that was known to be there. The explosion was so powerful that the mine caved in. Investigators later found twisted iron beams more than seven hundred feet away. Heavy equipment was found with burn marks.

Ironically, at the time of the explosion, W.E. Tytus, president of the Sunday Creek Coal Company, was giving a tour of the mine to some of the executives. The purpose of the tour was to showcase the new safety equipment. The president and the executives on the tour died along with the miners. In all, eighty-two men lost their lives in the disaster. This tragedy has created one of the most unusual hauntings in Ohio—one of sound. Sometimes people will hear an underground rumble with the muffled chaos of an explosion.[105]

The appearance of ghosts has often been connected with murder. Among those cases where such violence led to ghostly manifestations is one of the Mad Butcher—possibly the worst serial killer in Ohio's history. This unknown fiend was said by some to be Cleveland's answer to Jack the Ripper.

Like the infamous killer of White Chapel, the Mad Butcher found his victims in one poor neighborhood, the mean streets of the slum known as Kingsbury Run. As this was the height of the Great Depression, this district was crowded with dilapidated shacks and lean-tos until its end at the Cuyahoga River. With so many displaced people coming and going, it was the perfect hunting ground for a serial killer. Like Jack, the Mad Butcher mutilated the bodies of his victims, including decapitating people when they were still alive.

The horror began in 1934, when Frank La Gossie was wandering the beach searching for driftwood and discovered a human torso. The head and

Cleveland's haunted Kingsbury Run, hunting ground of the Depression-era serial killer known as the Mad Butcher. *Library of Congress.*

arms of the woman were missing, as well as the lower half of the legs. Soon another woman, this one decapitated, was found in the district. A year later, some children found the body of a man who was castrated and decapitated. Body after body was discovered in the same area, totaling thirteen.

One body was discovered because of the howling of a dog who was trying to paw its way into a basket left by a fence. A woman looked in the basket and told a neighbor that it contained bacon. The neighbor examined it for herself and, to her horror, announced that it was not bacon—the basket contained a human arm.

The people of Cleveland were understandably frightened, but they felt that they had the perfect solution in their new director of public safety. This was none other than the Untouchables leader himself, Eliot Ness. But tracking down a mad serial killer was quite different than fighting Chicago's gangsters. It was one thing to go after Al Capone and another thing to go after an unknown killer who cut off a man's head and then hid it in a pair of trousers a quarter of a mile away from the rest of the body.

Transients and others came and left Kingsbury Run quietly, and many people had no roots or family to contact. Ness knew that the killer was undoubtedly among the homeless who had shacks and tents in the area. He had the police raid the area, arresting the homeless people and burning the area to the ground. Then, like the Ripper murders, the crime spree stopped. Since those terrible days, the area has since been haunted by both the victims seeking justice and the killer still hunting for his next victim.

The *Cleveland Press* received a letter postmarked from California in 1939. It claimed to be from the Mad Butcher and stated that the murders were committed in the name of science.[106]

The horrifying tale of the Harrod Cemetery Hatchet Man comes from Bellefontaine. The grave of the serial killer who murdered two of his children and two wives has been seen to glow at night. It should be noted that the resting place of this man is unmarked.

One good story inspires another. While the unmarked grave is said to glow, the ghost of the Hatchet Man himself is said to haunt McArthur Township Road 56. He will still go after travelers, particularly ladies traveling alone, with his hatchet.

The dreaded Hatchet Man was a German immigrant named Andrew Hellman. His first wife, Mary, had three children before he became erratic and cruel. He disowned his son Henry, convinced that the boy was not his. As he fell further into madness, Andrew began to physically abuse the entire family.

Andrew Hellman's, a serial killer known as the Hatchet Man, has an unmarked grave. However, it is said to glow at times. *Photo by Douglas R. Weise.*

His children Louisa and John were apparently poisoned and died in 1839. Henry, who survived the poisoning, was sent to live with relatives, as Mary's brother was ill, and they needed help on the farm. When Rachel, Mary's sister-in-law, came to check on the family, she found that Mary was dead from being sliced in the head by a hatchet.

Andrew tried to convince people that strangers had broken in and murdered his wife, but no one was buying it. The authorities found that although he was covered in blood, he did not have as much as a scratch on himself. Apparently, he had smeared his wife's blood on him. The axe used to murder her was also found poorly concealed in a chimney. He was arrested, but before he was put on trial, he managed to escape.

He made his way to Baltimore, where under the alias of Adam Horn, he married a sixteen-year-old beauty named Malinda Hinkle. This new wife fared no better, as he used his hatchet again and even sliced up her body and hid parts throughout the house. One part of her was never recovered—her head.

He was arrested. This time he did not escape. He was tried, and on January 12, 1844, he was hanged. He struggled for four minutes—one minute for each of his victims—and then died. The one who picked up his body was none other than his son Henry, the boy he had disowned so many years before.[107]

Another rather grisly cemetery haunting comes from the tiny Moxahala Cemetery in Zanesville. This relates to the gruesome 1822 case of a young man who worked in a stable owned by Dr. Calvin Conant. The doctor had four medical students as apprentices. The stableman, Jake, was working in the barn when he saw a young woman's foot sticking out of the hay. Going to it, he moved the hay back to reveal the body of a dead girl.

Jake knew the girl—she was Miss Arnold from Putnam and had been very well known in the area. She had died of natural causes, most likely typhoid, a few days earlier and had been buried in the Moxahala Cemetery. Why was her dead body in the barn?

Needless to say, Jake panicked. He ran out of the barn and right into the four rather husky medical students. In a threatening way, they informed him that he was wrong—he had not seen a dead body under the hay, and he would certainly never tell anyone that.

The young man got the picture. The students were going out to the cemetery at night with shovels to acquire their study materials, and if he did not want to be the follow-up assignment, he better keep his mouth shut.

Moxahala Cemetery in Zanesville is a small open field with about nine gravestones still standing and at least two ghosts. *Photo by Douglas R. Weise.*

Left: The first name on this monument is Miss Arnold, the young woman whose body was stolen by grave-robbing medical students. *Photo by Douglas R. Weise.*

Below: Dr. Conant, who refused to help his students, had his own grave broken into. Like Miss Arnold, his ghost wanders Moxahala. *Photo by Douglas R. Weise.*

He did for a short time but finally could take it no longer and informed the authorities. They came to investigate the accusation of grave robbing but found only the clothes that the poor girl had been buried in. Of her body, there was not a single trace.

The medical students were arrested and even had to be smuggled out of town for fear that the horrified populace would lynch them. The defendants hoped that Dr. Conant would use his prominent position in the community to help them out of this little legal problem. They were out of luck. Dr. Conant swore up and down that he knew absolutely nothing about the matter and even signed an affidavit attesting to it. He faced no charges other than that of public opinion.

However, fortune did smile on the students. Apparently, in Zanesville, there was no law against grave robbing. Without physical evidence beyond the clothing, the charges were reluctantly dropped.

To this day, the spirit of the poor girl whose body was stolen and dissected wanders around as a shadow in the cemetery where her mortal remains should be lying at rest. She is not alone in her wandering. The ghost of Dr. Conant is also seen roaming around the grounds as if lost. Apparently, after he died, someone broke into his grave and scattered his bones around the grounds.[108]

Possibly one of the most accessible and pleasant haunted spots to visit in Ohio is the Moorish-style gazebo in Cincinnati's Eden Park. It is haunted by a lady in 1920s-style clothing who screams out, "No, Daddy, don't!" The ghost is that of Imogene Remus, wife of the notorious bootlegger and gangster George Remus.

George, a German immigrant from Berlin, began his career as a lawyer and pharmacist in Chicago. When Prohibition came along, he began defending minor gangsters who were making a great deal of money selling bathtub gin. Seeing that these uneducated lowlifes were becoming wealthy, he realized that he could use his business skills to create a considerable

The gangster's wife, Imogene Remus. Her ghost now haunts the Eden Park gazebo. *From the collection of the Public Library of Cincinnati and Hamilton County.*

The haunted gazebo in Eden Park, where gangster George Remus murdered his wife. *From the collection of the Public Library of Cincinnati and Hamilton County.*

bootlegging empire. But he could not do it in Chicago, where competing gangs were regularly using violence against one another.

So, he moved to Cincinnati and started his operation. He made the right choice, as his bootlegging empire stretched over several states—even back to Chicago. He became so wealthy that at a 1922 New Year's Eve party, he gave new cars to his guests as party favors.

However, such success could not last. He was arrested as a bootlegger and sent to the federal penitentiary in Atlanta. When he was released, he found that his wife, Imogene, had literally cleaned out their mansion, leaving him only one suit hanging in a closet. What made matters even worse was that the man she had run off with was Frank Dodge, the federal officer who had sent George to jail.

On October 6, 1927, the George and Imogene were in separate automobiles heading downtown to finalize their divorce. As the two cars approached the gazebo in Eden Park, George had his driver run his wife's cab off of the road. George then leaped out of the car brandishing a pistol. Imogene screamed, "No, Daddy, don't!" But it was too late. He fired at her, returned to the car and fled the scene. Imogene died at a nearby hospital.

Rather than fleeing, George decided that, as a lawyer, he could win this case. He turned himself in to the police and then went on trial as his own attorney. His opponent was a man with considerable legal background: Robert Taft, the son of the president and chief justice of the Supreme Court William Howard Taft.

George claimed temporary insanity. He had an ace in the hole: the people of Cincinnati hated Prohibition and loved George Remus. He was found not guilty and was released from a mental institution months later. Possibly due to this miscarriage of justice, the ghost of Imogene has been seen at the gazebo where she was shot, still begging for her life from the husband she had betrayed.[109]

In the Black Swamp area, we find the Precht Bridge over Turkey Foot Creek in Henry County. This span has a unique specter. It is a Native American warrior on a white horse, who, at certain times, will not permit the traveler to pass. Numerous people have seen this ghost and his horse over the years. Some say that he is guarding treasure. If he is, he has shown no interest in revealing its location.[110]

The story of the treasure involves a shipment of gold sheets en route to Fort Defiance to pay the troops of General "Mad" Anthony Wayne in the 1790s. The shipment was ambushed, and the gold ended up in an Indian village. By the 1830s, the American army was closing in, and the tribe decided that a change of address was advisable. They moved to Oklahoma, but thought it unwise to travel with their loot. They buried the gold somewhere along the Turkey Foot Creek and left someone behind to guard it. That guard is now a ghost but is still on duty. People have tried to find the booty but are invariably found the next day in a state of pure panic, swearing off treasure hunting forever.

Perhaps he is the same phantom horseman who has often been seen near the Henry County Cemetery. This specter was obliging enough to leave evidence of his existence. A man engaged in shoveling some sand near the graveyard saw the clear print of a horse's hooves in the sand one morning.

General "Mad" Anthony Wayne, Revolutionary War hero, won the Battle of Fallen Timbers and is now apparently Simon Girty's taskmaster. *Library of Congress.*

Speaking of General Wayne, he apparently has some pull in the afterlife. In the small town of Napoleon, he compels the ghost of "Renegade" Simon Girty to forever clean the general's cannons. The ghost of Girty has also been seen on Girty's Island in the Maumee River—first as a ball of light and then slowly turning into the notorious madman himself. Witnesses have even seen the tomahawk in his belt.

One of the great villains of colonial times, Girty was captured by the Seneca when he was young and was raised by them. He enjoyed their company and picked up some bloodthirsty practices. He later joined the American army in the Revolutionary War but deserted to the British. He encouraged and led Indian tribes on raids of American settlements and army patrols. He was not only present but also participated in the torture and death of Colonel William Crawford.

Under the circumstances, simply being forced to clean cannons is getting off rather light.[111]

One particular Cincinnati haunting might have been a complete hoax or the result of one of the ghastliest murders ever committed in the Queen City—the 1874 murder and immolation of Herman Schilling in the West End.

Schilling was caught sneaking into the bedroom of the daughter of a local tavern owner. The woman later died from cancer, and the father swore revenge on the illicit lover. Schilling was savagely beaten one night when he went to work at a local tanyard. Then, though he might have still been alive, his body was thrust into a furnace and burned.

It should come as no surprise that a ghost story would soon emanate from this scene of horror. Soon after the killers were arrested, a ghost was seen wandering the streets of the meatpacking district. By April, there were numerous eyewitness reports of a grisly phantom walking around in Gamble Alley near the tanyard, where the murder had taken place.

The wraith was described as a charred skeletal creature with a fire-blackened skull that, like Irving's celebrated Headless Horseman, could be detached and thrown at barking dogs or intruding humans. A number of locals, invariably emboldened by a good supply of beer, would occasionally go off in search of the phantom. Sometimes they would purportedly find what they were so foolishly looking for and would end the evening's ghost hunt running away in utter panic.

One of the people who decided to go in search of this specter was a gentleman named Schmidt. He was a drover, a man who not only drove herds of cattle or swine but also bought and sold livestock. He had just made

105

a particularly good sale and had more than $2,000 in his pockets. After buying a few rounds of drinks for the locals in the saloon, he announced to everyone present that he was going to do a little ghost hunting of his own. Of course, by now everyone in the tavern knew that he had a large wad of bills in his pocket.

What happened next is somewhat unclear. Schmidt marched through the drizzle and fog toward Gamble Alley, followed at a safe distance by a small parade of half-drunk men. Then the ghost reportedly made its appearance. The brave men bringing up the rear ran away as fast as they could, but for some reason, Schmidt was not with them.

When they finally regained their courage and their breath, they walked back to the alley searching for their companion. He was nowhere to be found. Whether he was murdered for the large amount of cash he so foolishly carried on his person (and heralded to everyone in a disreputable saloon) or was the victim of some supernatural agency, we will never know for certain.[112]

What greater violence could there be than war? Many battlefields throughout the nation have been said to be haunted with the appearance of lights. Ohio did not host many battles during the Civil War, but there was the 1863 case of Confederate brigadier general John Hunt Morgan leading his troop of raiders across the Ohio River and causing trouble throughout the Buckeye State. This act was a planned diversion, as Robert E. Lee had just led the army of Northern Virginia into Pennsylvania to divert troops from Grant's siege of the strategic river city of Vicksburg. Morgan's intention was to siphon off Union troops from going after Lee or helping Grant.

One of the several battlefields in which Morgan and the Yankees clashed was at Buffington Island in Meigs County. By July 19, the pivotal Battle of Gettysburg had been fought, turning Lee's army back to Dixie. Vicksburg had also been lost, essentially dividing the Confederacy in half. Morgan was now ending his raid and searching for a ford to get across the

Confederate raider General John Hunt Morgan caused havoc throughout southern Ohio, but his luck ran out when he tried to leave. *Library of Congress.*

Ohio River—but Old Man River had Yankee sympathies. The river was high and running fast, making crossing perilous.

The crossing was further delayed by a small group of militia. It was here that Morgan made his big mistake, delaying a day to allow his men to rest. When the battle was finally fought, he found himself facing Union ironclads and the troops of his pursuer, Brigadier General Edward Henry Hobson.[113]

While the battle is long over, ghostly soldiers have sometimes been seen running up hills. More often, a myriad of tiny lights is seen moving around the site of the clash. For them, the war will never be over.[114]

GHOSTS IN THE GRAVEYARD

Then the grave, that dark friend of my limitless dreams
(For the grave ever readeth the poet aright),
Amid those long nights, which no slumber redeems.
—*Charles Baudelaire, "Posthumous Remorse"*

What better place to find a ghost than floating about a graveyard? The following are some of the most interesting Ohio cemeteries whose residents just won't stay put.

A few cemeteries in Ohio have statues of angels that have been reported to weep. The meaning of the tears is debated. Some believe that to see the angel weep is an omen that it will soon be weeping for your death. However, other people state that it means that one's prayers have been answered. Soon there will be not a death but rather a healing of an illness or other miracle.[115]

Possibly the most famous of these statues is in Adams County in the small Winchester Cemetery. When visiting the Winchester Cemetery, look for a small circle of gravestones marking the burial place of a number of infants. Local folklore states that if one goes there after dark (which is illegal), you may hear children's voices whispering your name.

There is another weeping angel located in Athens, Ohio, at the West State Street cemetery. The cemetery is quite old, dating to pioneer times. Sadly, vandals have damaged many of the graves. The angel, dedicated in 1924 by Athens High School, is dedicated to those people buried at the grounds who are unidentified or forgotten. However, the angel does more

Winchester in Adams County is a small country town with a very strange angel in its cemetery. *Library of Congress.*

than just weep for the forgotten dead. It is also said to whisper to people who walk near it. There are even reports of the angel moving.[116] Beyond the weeping angel, people have also reported seeing balls of light floating around the grounds after dark.

One of the creepiest tales about a haunted cemetery involves the Old Egypt Cemetery in Flushing. The legend involves a truck driver who was driving by the graveyard too fast. He lost control of his rig and went down a hill in a fiery crash. In the midst of the accident, he lost not only his life but also his arm. To this day, the arm and hand crawl across the cemetery grounds seeking to be reunited with their former owner. One can sometimes hear the clicking of the fingernails against the gravestones as the hand moves relentlessly in its quest.

Talk of the arm and hand of the truck driver at Old Egypt Cemetery reminds one of another amputated limb haunting in Ohio. Coincidentally, the name of this place is Egypt Hollow Road, near Bainbridge in Pike County.

In the early 1800s, the townspeople had a celebration that included a bonfire. However, as sometimes happens in these situations, the timbers collapsed, showering fire on the bystanders. One of these was a young woman who was suddenly covered in fiery logs. People rushed to help her, but she was terribly burned. Worst among the injuries were the hands that were now burned to almost nothing but blackened flesh.

The town doctor had been attending the ceremony. Knowing that there was little chance of saving her life, he did the only thing he could to give her a small hope—he amputated both of her hands. After the operation, he gave the charred hands to his assistant to dispose of them. Not wishing to carry the ghastly things too far, the young man simply dumped them into a hollow tree stump.

Despite the best efforts of the doctor, the girl died from her injuries and burns. Since then, the discarded hands have sought to be reunited with the girl's body. The area where this happened is now Pike Lake State Park. However, if you wish to enjoy the trails, keep an eye on the path. The charred hands are said to be moving around on their own, like blackened spiders, and will sometimes grab at passersby. There have also been reports of phantom dogs rushing around the graveyard at night.[117]

There is a more fathomable ghost story from the Flushing area. Thirteen-year-old Louiza Catherine Fox and an older miner named Thomas Carr were lovers and intended to be married. However, Louiza's parents refused to consent to the union, concerned not only about the difference in age but also that Carr had a bad reputation and was often said to be violent.

Louiza dutifully broke off the engagement, which brought forth Carr's famous violent streak. He ambushed her as she walked home from her duties as a servant. He kissed her and then slashed her throat with a razor. It is best to do a crime like that without witnesses. Unfortunately for Carr, Louiza's brother was walking down the same street and saw his sister's murder and exactly who did it.

He gathered a group of men to go after his sister's killer. Carr attempted to commit suicide the next day—first by slashing his own throat as he had done to Louiza and then by shooting himself. He failed in both attempts and was soon brought to justice. March 24, 1870, was the day of the first legal hanging in Belmont County. Since then, the ghosts of both young people have been seen both in the cemetery (though Carr was buried by the courthouse and not in the Old Egypt Cemetery) and at the scene of the murder. A century and a half after her murder, people have not forgotten the bloodshed. Louiza Fox's grave is often decorated with the offerings of coins.[118]

Lincoln's funeral train is not the only specter that appears on schedule. In 1884, in the town of Miamisburg, near Dayton, the ghost of a young woman in white was seen wandering around the Village Cemetery. She

Right: Pike Lake State Park in Pike County is a gorgeous, secluded getaway. It also has a grisly haunting. *Photo by Douglas R. Weise.*

Below: While hiking the scenic trails of Pike Lake State Park, be wary of a severed hand crawling around in the brush. *Photo by Douglas R. Weise.*

would be seen walking at exactly at nine o'clock at night and seemed to have no awareness of any of the people who were watching her.

More and more people came to see the nightly haunting. Soon, with hundreds of people crowding into the cemetery every night, the neighbors were becoming annoyed. They pressured city officials to stop this nonsense. The officials decided that the best way to do this was to move all of the graves and rebury the people at the nearby Hill Grove cemetery, which had opened during the Civil War.

Though the graves were being moved, the ghost still continued to appear at exactly nine o'clock at night. Some people who got a good look at her stated that she looked like a member of the Buss family—a woman who had been murdered recently.

With the land converted into the Miamisburg Library Park, the ghost continued its nightly appearances. At the end of March that year, a group of men tried to attack the ghost with clubs and even shot at it. Needless to say, the ghost did not even look around, seemingly with no knowledge of what was transpiring in the world of the living.

The land of the former cemetery turned into a park is now the site of the Carnegie Library. The ghost has not been reported since the 1980s—a century after her first appearance. Apparently, like Lincoln's funeral train, this ghost has also faded away.[119]

Another haunting that attracted hundreds of witnesses was an eerie manifestation that occurred in the 1970s in the Evergreen Cemetery on South High Street in St. Paris. For some reason, at night, the gravestone marking the burial places of members of the McMorran family began to glow. One night, it is said that nearly one thousand people were present, and everyone saw the unearthly glow. Some have tried to blame it on some kind of glow-in-the-dark fungus, but so far, no debunking theories have held water. Curiously, like other ghostly manifestations, when one approaches the light, it dims.

Ohio has quite a few haunted cemeteries, including a few where ghosts will react if someone knocks on the door of the mausoleum or calls out to them. Some of the most famous of these ghosts are the Abbott family, buried in the Milan Cemetery on Broad Street in Milan. Benjamin and Lorena Abbott were some of the first settlers in region in the early 1800s. Their mausoleum features creature comforts, such as a rocking chair and some daguerreotype photos of the residents.

They are obviously quite comfortable in their eternal surroundings, for if one knocks on the door and disturbs their rest, they are said to charge

Originally a cemetery, Miamisburg is home to the ghost of a murdered girl who appeared nightly at exactly at nine o'clock, even after the cemetery was moved. *Photo Douglas R. Weise.*

out of the mausoleum and chase the intruder away. The geography of the cemetery already does a good job of keeping people away. The entrance to the tomb is facing away from the other graves, and one has to go down a steep ravine to a rather marshy area to reach the forbidden door.

Benjamin was buried in the vault in 1854. Two of his grandchildren are also buried in the same mausoleum, giving rise to the wild story that he murdered them and now guards their grave from intruders. This is not true, as they both, like so many children in those days, died from disease.

There are stories of a blue light flitting around the cemetery like a guard making a patrol. When the light comes to rest on a large cross near the mausoleum, the cross will begin to glow.

The Cedar Hill Cemetery east of Columbus has a number of haunts, including one that responds to knocking. The Baker mausoleum is protected by an iron door. But if one dares to knock on the door and then presses one's ears up to the entrance and listens very carefully, the person might hear faint screams from the past.

While you are in the cemetery, be sure to pay a visit to the famous Baby Face grave—a tombstone with the face of a baby carved into it. The local legend states that if you stare at the grave and its cherubic face and then turn

Knocking on the Baker mausoleum's door in the Cedar Hill Cemetery in Newark will supposedly elicit a response from inside. *Photo by Douglas R. Weise.*

The image on the eerie Baby Face grave in Cedar Hill reportedly changes position if one looks away and then back again. *Photo by Douglas R. Weise.*

around for about a minute and then turn back to the grave, something in it will have changed. Some say that the entire monument will change position.

One of the most obliging ghosts to those who knock on the door is found in the Salem Church Cemetery in Wellston. This is the ghost of a soldier who remains on permanent guard duty for the consecrated ground. The legend states that if one walks over to the old church door and knocks three times, the spectral guardian will allow you to hear him and know that he is not shirking his eternal duty. Investigators have picked up EVP recordings, and infrared photography has detected orbs and shadows in the building.

The soldier in question has not only been heard but also seen. He is dressed in a Union army uniform. The hauntings began around 1870, presumably when the veteran died. He is usually seen near the soldier's area.

In that same soldier's section, sometimes people see an entire group of soldiers standing at attention. The area is near the battlefield of Berlin Heights—the site of another conflict with Morgan's Raiders. Salem Church Cemetery is also home to the bodies of fallen Confederate soldiers.[120]

Another knock-answering spirit is found in the Hayden Mausoleum in Columbus. This ornate mausoleum contains the mortal remains of Charles H. Hayden. Charles, who died in 1920, was the son of the wealthy industrialist Peter Hayden. The elder Hayden began his career by producing materiel for the Union cavalry. After the war, he expanded his interests and invested in numerous enterprises, including coal, lumber, railroads and gas rights.[121]

Ohio has many cases of ghost lights, or orbs, appearing in haunted locations, such as cemeteries. One of these is in the Black Swamp region straddling the county line between Williams and Fulton Counties, the Golls cemetery. The mysterious orbs are sometimes seen zigzagging at high speed through the cemetery going between the gravestones. It is further related that one of the tombstones, a black one, always feels warm when touched.

A folk legend states that if one stands in front of Maryann Goll's tombstone, after a while, a ghostly mist will rise from the ground. It will then float over to the graves of her children, who died young. The visitor will then hear the sound of a woman weeping.

This cemetery is for the early pioneers. Besides the lights, Peter Goll and some members of his prominent family are sometimes seen taking a stroll through the graveyard that bears their name.[122]

Visitors to the Tyn Rhos Cemetery (whose name means "House on the Moor") near Thurman have often seen mysterious lights floating about the cemetery grounds. Inexplicable car problems have also been reported for those driving past the cemetery at night.[123]

There are also strange things going on at the Letart Falls Cemetery in Racine. Near the gate, one can sometimes hear the ghostly sobbing of an infant. Also, small balls of light are sometimes seen floating through the grounds.[124]

The Paul Peters Farm Cemetery in Lockbourne was used extensively during the terrible cholera epidemic in the mid-1800s, thus it is commonly called the old cholera cemetery. As so many people died ghastly deaths so quickly and well before their time, it should come as no surprise that the cemetery housing their remains would have reports of being haunted. This cemetery has reports of a shadowy figure wandering around the grounds at night, as well as scarlet balls of light floating about. There have also been reports of the sound of a scream. Those who have tried to investigate the strange goings-on in the graveyard have had electronic equipment fail for no reason. Some people have reported cold spots while walking through the grounds.[125]

The Cholera Cemetery in Sandusky is the result of what happens whenever a pestilent disease strikes. As it was in the days of the Black Death in the fourteenth century, people fearing that they would be the next ones to die fled the area. Of course, in regards to cholera, the disease had not yet shown symptoms in some cases. It would not take long before the refugees from Cincinnati, the port of entry for Ohio epidemics, would spread the disease as they fled seeking safety.

Lights have been seen floating around this cemetery. Voices have been heard, described by some as angry.[126] There is a good reason for this animosity. Amid the panic of dealing with a virulent epidemic and the rising number of corpses, people were often buried as quickly as possible with little or no memorial. In the confusion, there can be little doubt that a number of unfortunate people who appeared dead were actually buried alive.

People were so afraid of the disease (and rightfully so) that there was little care given to the grounds. Although it is one of the largest cholera cemeteries in the nation, it quickly became overgrown and neglected. It was not until 1924 that it was finally rehabilitated into the restful and well-preserved grounds that one sees today.

Another haunted cemetery is the Blanchard Cholera Cemetery in Blanchard. Reports in this spot usually describe the sound of ghostly laughter and weeping, particularly from children. As with the Paul Peters Farm cemetery, there are very few gravestones. People who died from this pestilent disease were buried quickly, and people usually stayed away from the graves.[127]

The Mound Cemetery in Marietta also has a ghostly blue light sometimes seen on the very top of the knoll. The earthwork is a Native American structure known as the Conus Mound. The cemetery built around it is one of the oldest in the Northwest Territory, dating to 1801. There is a debate as to whether these are merely ghosts of the soldiers buried in the grounds or spirit sentinels keeping watch over their comrades. Some people have seen the shadowy figure of a soldier on perpetual guard duty.[128]

The nearby Catholic cemetery on St. Mary's Street is also haunted by mysterious lights. Some children saw the lights and chased them with a flashlight. The lights promptly vanished.

The Beard Cemetery in Dundas, Vinton County, also has been haunted by ghostly lights. Besides these, a Civil War soldier is sometimes seen standing at attention near his grave. Some of the graves are even said to glow at times. This is a haunting that is a bit dangerous. Besides the lights and the soldier, there have been reports of people seeing a ghostly dog—and not a particularly friendly pooch. This hellhound with blazing apple-red eyes will sometimes chase people, forcing them to flee the grounds.[129]

The Great Mound of Marieta, where two cultures share the same space to bury their dead. *Library of Congress.*

This ghostly dog is not the only one haunting Ohio cemeteries. There are legends that in Cincinnati's magnificent Spring Grove Cemetery the spooky-looking Dexter Mausoleum may provide the sight of infernal canines. As the story goes, if one stands on the steps of the old sandstone chapel and looks to the north, then one might see a pack of white dogs running past. Some stories state that these white dogs would have one bit of color to them: blood-red ears.[130]

This immediately reminds anyone familiar with Celtic mythology of the spectral hounds known as the *cwn annwyn*, the same ones featured in the opening sequence "Pwyll, Prince of Dyved" in that mystical collection the *Mabinogion*: "And lo, as it reached the middle of the glade, the dogs that followed the stag overtook it and brought it down. Then looked he at the colour of the dogs, staying not to look at the stag, and of all the hounds that he had seen in the world, he had never seen any that were like unto these. For their hair was of a brilliant shining white, and their ears were red; and as the whiteness of their bodies shone, so did the redness of their ears glisten."[131]

The hounds that Pwyll encountered belonged to Arawn, a King of Annwn (the land of the dead). Are these the same ghost dogs that appear in Spring Grove Cemetery?

While you are looking around for phantom dogs in Spring Grove Cemetery, follow the white line in the road back into the cemetery to the grave of C.C. Breuer. It is located just as the road divides on top of a hill. The bust of his head on the monument is affixed with glass eyes. The urban legend states that no matter where you stand in front of the bust, the eyes will follow you. You may notice a number of footprints on the base of the statue, as young people have climbed up the side to get a good look at those weird eyes.

The statue isn't the only thing strange about this man. Mr. Breuer purchased his coffins in advance—one for him and one for his wife. The undertaker stored them for a while and then, for some reason, told him that if he wanted the coffins, he would have to store them himself. C.C., as he is commonly known, had no problem with this. He simply took delivery of the coffins and stored them underneath his and his wife's beds. How his wife felt about this macabre bit of home decorating has not been recorded.

In 1908, he wrote a suicide letter to the Hamilton County coroner, stating that he had difficulties with his children (he was once arrested for trying to commit arson on a building owned by his daughter) and did not like the government. "I am tired of living under our government," he told the coroner. "Consolidation means ruination. I therefor end my life to-night without the knowledge of anybody."[132]

IN SPRING GROVE CEMETERY, CINCINNATI, OHIO

James Key Wilson designed this mausoleum for Edmund Dexter, a Cincinnati whiskey baron. *From the collection of the Public Library of Cincinnati and Hamilton County.*

Urban legend states that if one stands on the steps of the Dexter Mausoleum, one might see ghost dogs running by. *Photo by Selena Rolfes.*

Left: Turn-of-the-century businessman C.C. Breuer slept with his coffin under his bed and tried to blow up a building. *Photo by Selena Rolfes.*

Below: The statue of C.C. Breuer's angry eyes fascinate visitors, who swear that they will follow you as you move. *Photo by Selena Rolfes.*

The coroner immediately dispatched two men to Breuer's Clifton home to check on him. He was fine.

The day before, it was reported that he had been arrested for attempting to blow up the Franklin Building at Third and Plum and was also carrying a concealed weapon. He requested psychiatric examination and was later confined to the mental hospital at Longview. He died that August of arterial sclerosis.

Besides ghostly lights, there are a number of Ohio cemeteries that have unusual hauntings. One of these is the Mount Blanchard Cemetery in Hancock County. A statue of a woman has curious effects when one touches the hand. Walking away, some people have reported hearing footsteps following them in the grass. Others have stated that the eyes of the statue turn glowing crimson.[133]

The Beech Grove Cemetery in Perry County is haunted by a sound. The ringing of the old church bell still calls the worshippers to prayer, although no living person has pulled the rope in decades. In fact, there is no rope, and indeed there no longer are any bells in the tower. Some people have seen certain graves glowing at night, and there are mysterious shadows seen gliding between the graves.[134]

As much as we would like to linger and pay our respects, we must now leave the cemeteries of Ohio and visit the things that go bump in the night.

9

POLTERGEISTS AND OTHER HAUNTS

And travellers, now, within that valley,
Through the red-litten windows see
Vast forms that move fantastically
To a discordant melody;
While, like a ghastly rapid river,
Through the pale door
A hideous throng rush out forever,
And laugh—but smile no more.
—Edgar Allan Poe, "The Haunted Palace"

The poltergeist, German for "noisy ghost," is one of the most frightening of hauntings. Rather than simply seeing a child on a staircase or a lady in white drifting through a bedroom, this unseen entity can make a family's life miserable. Often associated with the presence of a teen or preteen, this phenomenon often starts as a rapping and then grows to the movement of objects. As the entity grows in strength, items are often broken or even thrown at people. The famous Bell Witch poltergeist of Tennessee is credited with poisoning a man. Whether the poltergeist is a ghost, a demon, a psychic manifestation from the adolescent or a complete fraud is a question of debate; there is evidence to back each theory.

One of the most bizarre cases of poltergeist disturbance was in Cincinnati in the 1950s. Instead of a creepy mansion on a lonely road, this occurred in a very typical West End apartment building on Eighth Street just before the Eighth Street viaduct.

Dorothy Regler was a lady in her seventies and had lived for fourteen years in the apartment at 1020 West Eighth Street. During that time, there was nothing unusual occurring at the residence.

That is, until about five o'clock in the evening on Saturday, November 7, 1953. Mrs. Regler was in the apartment with her eight-year-old granddaughter, Ilean Sanders. All of a sudden, things started to move around on their own. Amid the confusion, the telephone and a tea kettle flew about, causing quite a disturbance. It did not calm down but became even more violent. Just outside of the apartment, the garbage cans and the wash wringer started to hop up and down. (Younger people may not be familiar with what a wash wringer looks like. Suffice it to say, these were rather large appliances.)

The garbage cans and the wringer were dancing about and managed to hop right up to the neighbor's door, a Mrs. Bertha Jackson. Quite naturally, she was curious about all of the commotion and opened the door to see what was going on. The items had bounced up against her door and seemed to be intent on entering her apartment. However, at the time, Mrs. Jackson was not receiving visits from inanimate objects. With a scream of horror, she slammed the door shut.

With things still moving wildly about the apartment, Mrs. Regler called the police. Cincinnati's finest arrived shortly thereafter and had absolutely no idea what to do. They certainly couldn't arrest anyone. One of the officers, apparently somewhat familiar with folk beliefs concerning spirits, took a box of salt and spread some of it on the floor by the threshold of the apartment door. However, folklore states that this is a device used to keep evil spirits from *entering* a dwelling by setting up a psychic barrier. Unfortunately, in this case, the spirits were already in the apartment, and that simply prevented whatever was in there from leaving.

Mrs. Regler could not stay in the apartment and spent the night on Liberty Street with Mrs. Savannah Love. The next day, Mrs. Regler and Mrs. Love went back to the apartment to see if the disturbances were still going on.

They were. The small stove kept hopping around of its own power and had moved to the center of the kitchen several times. No matter how many times the appliance was pushed back to its proper spot, it would move back to the center of the room. Things were still being tossed around. Little Ilean was struck by a flying breadbox. For some reason, the two women decided to take a close look at Ilean's doll. Without warning, the toy suddenly flew up and struck Mrs. Love.

By now, word had spread about the weird things happening on Eighth Street. Two days later, there were traffic jams and a very crowded sidewalk as more than five hundred people came to the area to catch a glimpse of some supernatural occurrence.

Members of Mrs. Regler's family rushed to be with her in her time of distress. One of these was her sister, Ora Lopez, who came from Chicago. She became quite angry at the masses of people who were thronging around her sister's apartment as though it were a circus sideshow. She threatened to give them a real phenomenon: a spray of water from a hose.

A University of Cincinnati professor of psychology, Dr. Charles Diserens, commented about the strange goings-on. He put the cause at telekinesis, although he was at a loss to explain exactly how this came about and what the working of it was.

Eventually, the unnatural activities ceased, and life returned to normal for Mrs. Regler.[135]

Not too far from the Freeman Avenue poltergeist, a decade later, there was another noisy ghost occurrence right up the road in the old neighborhood of Price Hill. A family living in a one-hundred-year-old house started to feel the effects of a haunting. There were strange sounds, including the sound of boots on the stairs. It even included the classic haunting sound of the rattling of chains, as if Jacob Marley had dropped in for a visit. A single room on the third floor had a frigid area—the classic cold spot. All attempts to heat it failed.

The family tried to communicate with the spirit using a series of knocks. The ghost obliged and informed them that he was a man who had died in the house.

Once, a member of the family took a book on Buddhism off of the shelf. This apparently displeased the resident spook, who immediately let out a deafening roar. Finally, the family had enough and moved out. But as sometimes happens, the family was at their new address when they received a telephone call. It was the voice of a gruff man, who informed them that he knew where they were.

Poltergeists, once attached to a family rather than a particular dwelling, have been known to follow people to different, previously unhaunted addresses.[136]

One of the most famous cases of a modern poltergeist is the Columbus disturbance of 1984. John and Joan Resch, along with their adopted teenage daughter, Tina, were under attack from what appeared to be a poltergeist. As a great deal of damage was being done, the family contacted their insurance agent, Rein Gellner of the Tice Insurance Agencies. The Resch family was covered by Midwestern Indemnity. The claim was filed, and for a while,

Price Hill from Lick Run Valley, Cincinnati.

Many old Price Hill buildings are still standing, along with a few ghosts. *From the collection of the Public Library of Cincinnati and Hamilton County.*

no one knew exactly what to do with it. Was poltergeist activity covered by homeowner's insurance?

In the meantime, glasses and dishes at the household were being broken, appliances were going on and off on their own, and all manner of damage was being sustained. As had happened in the Regler case, a mob of people were gathering outside to catch a glimpse of some supernatural activity. Among the crowd was the skeptic and paranormal debunker James Randi. He requested permission to come in to investigate but was told no.

Journalists, however, were allowed in, and one left a camera where it was unnoticed but still filming. Amid the confusion, the camera caught Tina causing a bit of the damage herself. Shortly thereafter, the insurance claim was withdrawn by the embarrassed family.[137]

Another poltergeist in Columbus occurred in 1976. These people wisely did not want their names revealed. A man who was studying to be a minister suddenly found his house haunted by something that started off by moving things around in the kitchen. His girlfriend stated that something invisible touched her on the rear end. To make matters even more embarrassing for a divinity student, this poltergeist liked pornography. This rather lustful specter liked one particular movie so much that it kept ordering it. The man was billed for turning it on ten times in a two-week period.

The family dog, of course, was freaked out and did not want to stay in the house. He was replaced by a border collie who simply considered the ghost to be one of the family. Being a border collie, it wanted to herd everything, whether they were flesh and blood or spirit. After a while, the haunting ended.[138]

Some Ohio haunted locations have ghostly manifestations that can affect physical objects—an area that borders on the poltergeist. For example, there is a great deal of ghostly activity in Shawnee State University, particularly in the Verne Riffe Center for the Arts. Poltergeist activity includes books flying off of shelves. One can often hear (but not see) children either running through the hallways or whispering and giggling. If one listens long enough, they might hear ghostly music playing.[139]

Let us now end this examination of the ghost lore of Ohio with some random but notable hauntings.

Possibly the most delightful ghost one can encounter in the Buckeye State was found in Greenfield in Highland County during the 1800s. It was a pretty young woman who loved to sneak up on young men and kiss them. She was seen in the plot of land designated the Pioneer Cemetery, or simply the Old Burying Ground.

In 1881, the *New York Times* carried an article about the ghost. It mentioned the encounter of a young man named Smithers. The ghost snuck up behind him and kissed him. As he was an assistant pastor at a Baptist church, he was in no mood for a romantic rendezvous with the dead. He broke away. Two nights later, a young man named Edward Potter was similarly accosted. For Potter, this was his first kiss from a girl. He was kissed three times before he realized that it might be best not to start one's love life by smooching a dead girl. In 2010, a parade in Greenfield featured a float with a grave marker and, of course, a pretty girl blowing kisses to the crowd.[140]

There is a rather curious haunting closely related to the doppelgänger found in the historic Golden Lamb Inn and Restaurant in Lebanon. Sarah Kilpatrick lived there when she was young and apparently really liked the place. Her family moved out, and she grew up normally. However, her ghost haunts the inn, not as the adult she grew into but rather as a child who loved the inn.[141]

Sarah's specter is not alone, for there are two other ghosts in the building—one quite famous. There is a second child ghost, Elizabeth Clay, who died of typhoid on the premises in 1825.

The other ghost would be immediately recognized by anyone familiar with antebellum history. This is Clement Laird Vallandigham. This Ohio

Lebanon's historic Golden Lamb restaurant and bed-and-breakfast has several ghosts who never checked out, including Clement Vallandigham. *Library of Congress.*

congressman was what was known at the time as a "Copperhead," a Northerner who was a staunch supporter of slavery and the right of the South to secede.

At one point during the war, Vallandigham was arrested by the Union army and exiled to a foreign nation—the Confederate States of America. Even though this was illegal, and the United States did not recognize the legitimacy of the Confederate government, Vallandigham was duly handed over to the Confederate army.

In 1871, he and some other attorneys were in a room in the Lebanon House (the current Golden Lamb). To demonstrate how his client, on trial for murder, could not have committed the crime, he made a demonstration using himself as the subject. His theory was erroneous, as he accidently shot himself and soon died. His ghost is still walking the halls of the Golden Lamb, probably muttering, "Well, that didn't quite go as planned."[142]

Supernatural entities, particularly ghosts, often appear in what may be considered in-between spots. When a house is haunted, the ghost is often seen on stairs—places that are on neither one floor nor another. They are very often seen in windows—spots that are in the house but bordering on the outside.

Elevators, as well as regular stairways, are places where spirits might manifest. The freight elevator in Cincinnati's Music Hall often has a mind

Left: The Golden Lamb's most famous ghost is the Ohio Democratic congressman Clement Vallandigham, an outspoken opponent of the Civil War. *Library of Congress.*

Right: Clement Vallandigham, leader of the Copperhead movement, is buried in Dayton's beautiful Woodland Cemetery, where there are several other reported hauntings. *Photo by Douglas R. Weise.*

of its own. The one in the public library in the Athens County town of Nelsonville has also been known to run with no one in it or operating the controls. Things are sometimes inexplicably moved around in the building.

The majestic Masonic Temple on West Riverview Avenue in Dayton has a similar problem with its elevator. Apparently, one of the Masons didn't want a little thing like dying to interfere with his fraternal activities. In fact, the ghost has been seen wandering about the halls on the third floor.[143]

Another ornate Dayton building with a retinue of ghosts is the Memorial Hall on East First Street. One can occasionally hear high heels clicking down empty corridors. Lights turn on and off by themselves. Some people who have played pool have glimpsed a man in old-fashioned clothing watching their game. One of the ghosts is believed to be a janitor named Drake who fell to his death in the orchestra pit.[144]

Music Hall was built over a potter's field. Renovations frequently unearth human remains. *From the collection of the Public Library of Cincinnati and Hamilton County.*

The magnificent Masonic Temple in Dayton, home to some very outgoing spirits. This one plays with elevators. *Photo by Douglas R. Weise.*

Close-up of the door of the Dayton Masonic Temple, showing the lion head door knockers. *Photo by Douglas R. Weise.*

Another location seemingly haunted by a noisy ghost is a pair of old buildings located right next to each other at 111 North Columbus Street in Lancaster. The businesses on the ground level include Kool Beans and the Paperback Exchange. The phenomena feature the usual rapping and banging, disembodied voices and things moving about on their own or disappearing only to be found later in an unlikely spot.[145]

The "official theater in Ohio," the Ohio Theatre in Columbus, has a ghost that loves to play pranks on people. One of its favorite activities is turning lights on and off. The people who work there know this ghost as Charlie, who, in the 1970s, was the stage manager. (Some accounts say he was a stagehand who died in the middle of a performance sometime in the 1950s.) Though he blows light bulbs by turning them on and off, one cannot doubt that Charlie is a gentleman. He has been known to hold the elevator door open for ladies.[146] He is not alone in his haunting, as this theater has two other ghosts: a woman who likes to stay in the balcony and a spectral child in the basement.

Curiously, there is another theater in Ohio with the same name and similar haunts. The Ohio Theater in Mansfield also has a ghostly woman on-site. She was seen dressed in mourning black walking across the stage.[147]

Why do ghosts like to play with lights? There are numerous instances of ghosts causing electric lights to flicker on and off. One of these is in the southeastern Ohio city of Coal Grove. Here one will find the Monitor School, named after the Monitor Pig Iron furnace that was located there. The building that one sees today replaced the traditional little red schoolhouse that was built in 1857. People passing by the school at night have seen strange orbs of lights floating around in the darkened rooms. But not all of the rooms are dark, for lights have also been known to flicker on and off for no reason.[148]

Somewhat related is a curious ghost haunting Orton Hall at Ohio State University. It is supposedly the spirit of a savage man with primitive features—the stereotypical Neanderthal with a humped back and oversized forehead. (It should be noted that science has demonstrated that the Neanderthal did not look the way they are presented; the original fossils were of a man deformed by arthritis.)

Orton Hall is also the location of many reports of poltergeist activity from someone—primitive or not. Lights go on after they have been turned off, doors slam or open and, in 1986, someone or something walked off with an entire Christmas tree.[149]

Left: The ornate Ohio Theater in Columbus has a ghost nicknamed Charlie who plays jokes and turns lights off and on. *Library of Congress.*

Below: Dr. Isaac Fowler died while crossing the bridge in the 1800s. His ghost is often heard in the area making loud noises. *Library of Congress.*

Certainly, one of the most frightening Ohio haunts is a tale that could have come out of a country music song. In the winter months of 1952, a number of truck drivers traveling on old U.S. 40 in the vicinity of the Taylorsville and Englewood Dams gave terrifying reports of a crazy driver on the road who rushed straight toward them. Since they were in a truck, they did not have a lot of room to maneuver. Fortunately, the car turned off at the last minute, avoiding a head-on crash. But the truck drivers could see the man behind the wheel playing a deadly game of chicken with them. It was a skeleton. Shortly after that, as so often occurs in cases of multiple supernatural encounters, the reports just stopped.[150]

While we're on the road, one of those in-between places where people sometimes see supernatural entities are bridges. They are on neither shore but are suspended in space over water and air. Supernatural creatures might be on the span or might live beneath, as is the case with the Scandinavian trolls. Ohio may be short on trolls, but it does have quite a few haunted bridges.

Those in Zanesville who live near the Y Bridge are used to hearing a series of bangs in the night, particularly if it is foggy. The old-timers assure people that this is the ghost of Doc Isaac Fowler, a country physician in the 1800s. He was on his way to help a seriously ill patient one night when he lost control of the horse on the Y Bridge. He and the horse went over the side. For this reason, he is also sometimes referred to as the Licking River ghost.[151]

Chief among these legends is the folktale of the Crybaby Bridge. This is a relatively new bit of folklore, spread mostly by teenagers who wish to visit these places at night to see the supernatural. While in ages past, folklore was spread by word of mouth, nowadays, these stories are transmitted—and embellished—by the internet.

Pretty much every state in the union has at least one Crybaby Bridge, and Ohio has two dozen. These stories often involve a group of teens who went off of the road at a bridge, with at least one if not all dying; a distraught, often pregnant teenage girl jumping off of the bridge after being spurned by her boyfriend; or an unwed mother tossing her baby over the side of the bridge. The folklore states that those who go to the bridge will possibly hear the crying of the baby or the wailing of the mother.

A variation of this is the modern folktale of the car stuck on the railroad tracks. If one stops a car on the tracks and has a good supply of baby powder spread on the back hood, children's handprints will appear trying to push the car off of the same tracks that they died on. However, as trains do use the tracks, this would definitely fall under don't try this.[152]

Zanesville's Y Bridge, built after Doc Fowler's death, is just one of more than a dozen haunted bridges in Ohio. *Library of Congress.*

For some reason, Ohio has more than its share of these crybaby bridges. Perhaps the most famous is the one in the exceedingly haunted area known as Rogue's Hollow near Akron. This small bridge crossing Silver Creek is the spot where an unwed mother tossed her baby to die in the waters below. Not only can one hear the cries of the baby but might also see the mother of the child lamenting her rash act.

A more dramatic telling of this tale has the young woman being accused of witchcraft. The people in the nearest town, Doylestown, said to protect the child they would take it away from her and raise it in a Christian home. The accused witch decided to thwart them by killing the child by throwing it into the frigid waters of the Silver Creek.

However, as one always finds in folklore, there is a variation of this story. In it, a car slid off of the bridge, and all of the occupants died immediately except the baby. The baby starved to death and now haunts the area.[153]

The Crybaby Bridge in Lorain County is on Highway 34 near Vermilion, where, if one is near enough, the crying of a baby can be heard. Tiny handprints can sometimes be seen on the car after crossing the bridge. This small bridge is located near a hillside where the Light and Hope Orphanage once stood. Opened in 1910, it was operated by Reverend John Sprunger. There were, as would be expected, tales of cruelty against the children. Besides the crying, one can sometimes hear the laughter of children.

At the intersection of Darrow and Barrows Roads, one can sometimes hear the ghostly screeching of tires.[154]

Of all of the in-between places that one can see a ghost, perhaps the most in-between is a mirror. Mirrors have fascinated people for years, apparently giving us a glimpse of an impossible backward world—the same one that Alice fell into. Mirrors have been used to see into the future (Nostradamus used a variation of this) and are also said to sometimes capture the souls of the dying, thus mirrors are typically covered in a house after a family member has passed.

One ghost that seems to be trapped in mirrors is a young Civil War soldier who haunts the Circleville Memorial Hall. Many people over the years have seen him in the looking glasses. So many have encountered him staring back at them that he has been given a nickname: Charlie. Apparently, he is somewhat fascinated by the modern convenience of indoor plumbing. He continually flushes toilets in the building.[155]

Let us end our look at Ohio ghosts with a musical haunting from Cincinnati in the Gilded Age. In a frustrating 1875 case in which names were once again not supplied, the haunted house was an elegant mansion inhabited by "a very popular and wealthy citizen....A man once noted for his skepticism in matters spiritualistic."[156] Sadly, this is all of the description that we have of the family.

The teenage daughter of the family became ill, and the father's wealth could not save her. Sadly, she died, leaving the family and the household servants in mourning. However, a while after the period of sadness, just when life would begin to return to the new normal, it was discovered that the daughter was not quite as departed as she should have been.

At first, the servants noted that there were cold spots throughout the grand house. Some of the maids heard the rustling of an invisible silk dress walking down the hallways, accompanied by the cold spot. Then came the most bizarre phenomenon—a weird activity that soon caused one frightened young maid to quit her position.

Apparently, the daughter loved to play the piano. After her death, the instrument was closed up and locked. However, now, in the middle of the night, forlorn piano music would occasionally be heard from the parlor. Everyone in the household heard the mournful sonata, which was described as being "distinct, skillful, yet had something drowsily weird about it."[157] Those brave enough to venture near the room when the ethereal concert was going on would state that the air was icy, as if someone had left a window open in the middle of the coldest February night.

In the reassurance of daylight, the family and servants finally found the nerve to venture into the sealed chamber. They found the piano still locked as it had been immediately after the girl's death. When the family unlocked it, they looked at the keys. They still had dust on them, undisturbed by living fingers.

FROM SUMMERLAND
TO THE BUCKEYE STATE

The ghosts evoked by our modern medium wizards are but very feeble ghosts indeed; they can only make their presence apparent by a peculiar process termed materialization; they can only materialize with great labor and anguish and having materialized, they are wholly dependent upon the medium's mercy for even such ephemeral existence. Furthermore, they can excite no fear, nor can they gain any reverent respect from the living by reason of their supernatural powers. In brief, it may be stated that the ghosts of Spiritualism are domesticated, and harmless by reason of their domestication.[158]

In an ironic twist, a group of people whose preoccupation was to contact ghosts turned into ghosts themselves. The tale of Utopia, Ohio, is a wild one. Located in Clermont County along Route 52, the area was originally settled as a religious commune by a preacher named Charles Fourier. His followers trusted him to create a bit of paradise on earth, thus the name of the settlement, Utopia.

Fourier taught that God was about to usher in a wonderful age of peace and prosperity destined to last for thirty-five thousand years. His grip on reality was somewhat tenuous, as he also held that during this time period, all of the oceans would be turned into lemonade.

Like most communes based on religious communism, people became disillusioned and could not live in harmony. All work and the fruits of the labor were supposed to be distributed equally—a sure recipe for anger and bickering. A man named Josiah Warren took over and, despite being an anarchist, instituted such radical ideas as private property. Notwithstanding these moves, the commune could not survive. In December 1847, the land was sold to John O. Wattles, leader of a group of spiritualists. This was when the tragedy struck.

The people of the area urged Wattles to not build their meetinghouse so close to the banks of the Ohio River, stating that the many floods usually went well over the land on which they were working. Wattles ignored their advice and built the structure—apparently in the flimsiest manner possible. It was a disaster waiting to happen, and it didn't have to wait long.

On the thirteenth of that same month, despite a raging storm and a rapidly rising Ohio River, the society was gathered in the building to have a celebratory dance. They had not danced for long when the south wall of the structure was suddenly torn away by frigid river water rushing in. Many of the spiritualists were washed away. Of the 156 people in the building that night, only six survived.

Numerous ghosts are seen near the site of the disaster, including strange lights, misty shapes on the water and sometimes full apparitions of people soaking wet in old-fashioned clothing emerging from the water. The Wattles house, built more solidly, is nearby. Ghosts have been reported there as well, including a group of wet spiritualists entering the house and suddenly vanishing. Dogs do not want to enter the building.[159]

An intriguing feature of this site is the presence of one and possibly two bizarre places of worship, no doubt from Josiah Warren's movement. This would be an underground church. Not as well known is another strange temple, once again placed under the surface of the earth. Ron Hill, a Clermont County historian, described it: "About half a mile further up the road is a man-made cave back into the hill side (about 30 ft. deep) that has architecture features very similar to the 'underground church.' No one seems to know anything about it. I believe it was also built by the same people that built the 'church.'"[160]

Underground temples are rare but have been around since prehistoric times. They have been found from China to Colombia. One, known as the Mithraeum, was found underneath the Circus Maximus in Rome.

In the Victorian era, spiritualism became an ever-growing movement, attracting devoted followers and causing a great deal of outrage among traditional Christian churches. While the new zealots were convinced that they were experiencing the secrets of the universe, traditional denominations pointed out the numerous prohibitions against this practice throughout the Bible.

To better understand this practice, let us take a quick look at a detailed account of a typical séance conducted in the Gilded Age. In March 1883, a number of people, including a reporter for the *Cincinnati Enquirer*, gathered in the Smith residence on Chase Avenue in the Cincinnati suburb of Northside for a séance. It was there that a well-known murdered man made his dramatic appearance as a ghostly master of ceremonies. According to the reporter, "It may be proper to remark that Harry Baldwin, the young man whose mysterious murder several years ago excited so much comment, is the controlling spirit, all the manifestations being under his personal supervision."[161]

This was the famous unsolved crime in Gilded Age Cincinnati. In 1879, the police found a prominent insurance agent, Harry Baldwin, leaning against a wall in an alley off Elm Street. His voice was slurred, and he was incoherent. Thinking that he was only drunk, they took him to a nearby police station to sleep it off. Hours later, someone realized that rather than sobering up, he was dying. A doctor was summoned, recognized him and proclaimed that he wasn't drunk—he had been shot. The doctor was unable to save his life, leading to the ongoing mystery and scandal.

At the beginning of the séance, the twelve participants (the newspaperman made thirteen) were thoroughly searched, particularly for flowers and fish. In the last gathering, the departed Harry Baldwin had promised to provide these items for the participants at their next gathering. For this reason, there was a fishbowl with one goldfish swimming in it. The articles used in the séance, including the famous megaphone device known as a trumpet (through which the spirits would supposedly speak), were also available for the reporter's examination.

Séances are always conducted in utter darkness, and this one was no exception. Not only was a heavy, solid grate placed in front of the fireplace, but also a heavy blanket was suspended from the mantel to make absolutely certain that there would be no visible light. The medium was John Garrison, the son-in-law of Caleb Lingo, a man well known in the Northside area, who now has a street named for him in the neighborhood. Caleb and his brother were the owners of a local sawmill.

The ceremony, despite the fact that the practice is expressly forbidden in several passages in the Bible, was begun with a quick prayer. After this, the six ladies in the group sang a short hymn. As soon as the women finished their song, there was a rustling around the trumpet and other items. The spirits were becoming impatient. Just as quickly, the voice of the murdered Harry Baldwin was heard, promising everyone present that there would be numerous manifestations that evening. All were excited as the proceedings moved along.

Almost immediately, the promised cut flowers appeared, falling from the sky like heavenly manna. Along with this, sparkles of light, the classic will-o'-the-wisps of folklore, sometimes known as corpse lights, appeared, flitting around the darkened chamber.

No sooner did the floral rain cease than there was a spectral concert. Not only did the trumpet play but also a guitar, both of which floated in the air. A heavy dulcimer joined in as well. However, the spirits became frustrated at a fife, which they could not play and threw to the floor. Apparently, one needs breath to play a fife, yet they somehow managed to make sound with a trumpet.

A music box played eerie melodies as it too floated about the room and, for a moment, landed on the hand of the reporter. He tried to take hold of it, but the machine whisked away in the darkness.

A number of prominent deceased people spoke to the assembled spiritualists, including one president, James Garfield, who had been assassinated two years earlier. Also in attendance was the recently deceased Alexander Stephens, the former vice-president of the Confederate States of America. As always seems to happen in a séance, there was the appearance of the voice of an Indian chief. This one was named Swift Foot. When the lights returned, it was found that instead of one goldfish there were now three swimming in the little glass bowl.

The reporter was able to ask Harry Baldwin a question. He chose to ask how the spirits could enter the house when all of the doors and windows were sealed. The reply was that such barriers made no obstacle to spiritual beings. Perhaps the strangest part of the séance is that the diligent *Enquirer* reporter sitting there amazed at the phenomena around him never bothered to ask Mr. Baldwin who had murdered him in 1879.

Harry left a message on a slate in which he alluded to his murder and his present state: "I am not dead, but living; not in the mortal form that now lies in the casket beneath the clay, but clothed in an immortal garb in a home beyond the grave, not so far but that I can return and see my ever dear and loving home....When she [his wife] realized that I had been cut down as wheat by the husbandman by an unmerciful hand, she, like the lily of the valley, with a drooping head, faded away with a heart full of anguish."[162]

Hattie Baldwin had died of pneumonia a year and a month after her wedding, the day after their only child was christened. The funeral at the Unitarian church had been so overwhelmed by curious spectators that hundreds of people had to remain outside.

Of course, even if the reporter had asked who killed Harry Baldwin, no name would have been given. The medium had no idea who committed the crime—no more than did the police.

Any reasonably cynical observer would have seen through the whole charade of the séance. If the same reporter had witnessed a stage magician at a carnival sideshow producing fish in a bowl, there would have been mild clapping, perhaps a comment, "Boy, he's good." But he would not have believed that the prestidigitator had an open line of communication with Summerland and had brought back living fish from the land of the dead. (Perhaps the reporter should have asked for a tuna instead of a goldfish.)

Even a third-rate amateur magician would have known to spread powder on the floor—powder, which when the lights went on, would have revealed a series of footprints from where the ninja-clad assistants wandered around the completely darkened room tossing flowers on the ladies, picking up and playing musical instruments and, of course, the famous trumpet.

There is one major difference between the stage conjuror with his magically appearing goldfish and the medium in the darkened room. When the act is over, the magician will simply take his bow, enjoy the applause and leave. He will not take a large fee from a bereaved widow or the parent of a beloved son who had died in the Battle of Antietam, asking for more and more money. The stage magician will never dream of telling people that their money has a curse on it and must be brought to him to have the curse removed. (This old scam still works today. When the victim opens the envelope later, they will invariably find, instead of their money, a mass of newspaper. The medium departed in haste for a long journey out of town and the jurisdiction.)

Thus before proceeding any further on the subject of spiritualism, it should be emphasized in the strongest possible terms that to visit a medium and pay for the services of conjuring the dead is worse than walking through a bad part of town with fifty-dollar bills protruding from one's pocket. In both cases, being robbed is inevitable; however, in the bad part of town, the thief will only take what is on the victim at the time. Those who engage the medium might lose their entire life savings.

The modus operandi behind the simple parlor tricks of mediums, often including the use of a common cheesecloth as ectoplasm, are readily available to anyone who wants to look for them. At the very least, before engaging in any such activity, the soon-to-be-victim is strongly encouraged to read *The Psychic Mafia* by a reformed medium, M.L. Keene.[163]

While we may think that spiritualism began in 1848 with the Fox sisters in Hydesville, New York, conversing with Mr. Splitfoot through a series of raps, in truth, the practice of communicating with the spirit world is perhaps the oldest religion known to man. We find mention of spiritualism in the writings of the third-century philosopher Iamblichus, the church father Eusebius and many others throughout the ancient world. The popularity of this practice is demonstrated by the numerous biblical writings that condemn it.

The most famous medium in the ancient world is the woman known as the Witch of Endor, mentioned in 1 Samuel 28:3–25, who summoned the spirit of the prophet Samuel to predict the outcome of a battle for King Saul. There is something rather curious about this passage that most commentators have overlooked. The witch, often identified as a woman named Sedecla, continually asks Saul to eat some of her food. While on the surface this invitation may seem trivial, it actually tells us a great deal about the nature of this witch.

Ancient belief states that denizens of the spirit world would have power over their victims if they could persuade them to eat their food. This is seen in the classical myth in which the kidnapped Persephone is bound to Hades when she eats a solitary pomegranate. This is also referred to in the Celtic tale in the *Mabinogion* "How Cyfwlch Loved Olwen" and in Miyazaki's anime classic *Spirited Away*. Thus this witch of Endor may have been more than just a mortal woman or was definitely in the service of evil spirits. Either way, it did not go well for King Saul.

The whole popular movement of spiritualism may have been started by the two Fox sisters, Maggie, who was fifteen at the time, and eleven-year-old Katy, making noises in the night to frighten their mother. Their father, who was known to be superstitious, believed that their house was haunted, reportedly with an entity dubbed by the girls as Mr. Splitfoot, a reference to the cloven-hooved devil.

While the sisters may not have been genuine mediums, there is little doubt that they were good merchandisers. Excitement and word about the haunted Fox house spread quickly. A year later, the Fox sisters gave their first public demonstration of their "supernatural abilities" at the Corinthian Hall at nearby Rochester. From there, they entered in a stormy life of fame and notoriety as stage spiritualists.[164]

The popularity swept the country, and then an event came, which, despite the condemnation of clergy from all Christian faiths, cemented the practice in the fabric of American society. A dozen years after Mr. Splitfoot made his appearance, the nation was ripped apart by the Civil War. Around 750,000 Americans died as a result of the brutal conflict, leaving behind a multitude of grieving parents, spouses and siblings. This was the perfect time for spiritualism to emerge from the parlor to become a major force in American society—not to mention giving hucksters a chance to fleece the grieving loved ones of young men who gave their lives in places like Gettysburg, Franklin, Shiloh and countless other blood-soaked fields throughout the nation.

Spiritualism had become so popular during the Civil War that there was even a major newspaper issued by the practitioners, with the pretentious title *Banner of Light*. This weekly newspaper began in Boston in 1857. However, as spiritualism exploded in popularity, the operation required a second journal to cover the messages from Summerland directed to the people of the Midwest. The publishers looked for a western state that was friendly and welcoming to those who communicated with the dead. In 1866, they found their haven: Ohio.

When spiritualism became an organized church, some of its adherents became rather fanatical. The devotees were often true believers and could become rather testy about those who criticized their curious practices.

As early as 1856, one such devotee wrote a long and rambling letter to the *Cincinnati Enquirer*, denouncing those who derided the faithful and attempting to explain the mechanics of his beliefs: "We are not in the least chagrined at your denunciations...for we once did the same, but then we were, as you are now, wholly ignorant of the subject matter....We read the slurs of the secular press and the denunciations of the theological with a like indifference... knowing that the time is not far distant when truth will vindicate itself."[165]

He continued, stating not only his right to believe what he wishes, but also that it is absolutely true: "Our religion is not, properly, a faith, as is that of other religionists, but it is a knowledge, because we know it to be true and have it sustained by evidence, against which nothing can possibly prevail."

After speaking of the evidence of spirit communication, he attempted an explanation of how the universe works: "There is no such thing as a void in nature....All space is filled with substantial matter. This matter, however, is divided into two grand divisions, one of which Spiritualists call external, and other internal matter. The substances which compose the earth, the sun, moon and stars, with all their contents, whether solid or gaseous, we shall call non-electrical; while the matter that fills all the spaces that intervene between them, and, at the same time, penetrates them all to their centers, we shall call electrical. This latter is the spirit world. It is composed of electrical matter, which is substantial materiality, but is imperceptible to our external senses."[166]

The letter rambles on and on, trying to sound scientific and learned but, in truth, making almost no sense whatsoever.

Fifty years later, the famed magician Harry Houdini would spend a great deal of time unmasking these practices. He even wrote a bestselling book exposing the simple magician tricks used by mediums.

Many spiritualists in the Gilded Age delighted in stating the tired refrain that Abraham Lincoln and Queen Victoria were both devout spiritualists. In the case of Abraham Lincoln, this often-repeated claim was simply not true. His presence at séances in the White House is, to this day, cited by spiritualists as an endorsement of their practices. However, looking at the actual record, it is apparent that the Great Emancipator was not a believer in talking to the dead—but his wife, Mary Todd, was. She was grieving over the death of their son Willie. In this mix of grief and depression, a medium named Nettie Colburn had snaked her way into Mary Todd's life.[167]

The sixteenth president, who at the time was rather busy with other matters, did what he could to protect her from being swindled. Sometimes the president would attend, not as an adherent but rather to make sure that his wife was not being cheated. There is even the curious case in which a ghost supposedly made a piano move around a room of the White House. Lincoln jumped onto the instrument to make it stop moving but reportedly wound up being taken for a ride.

He was correct in his apprehensions. After his assassination, Mary Todd Lincoln was indeed victimized by mediums. It became so dreadful, and her mental health deteriorated so severely, that in 1875, her son Robert took her to court to have her committed to a mental asylum. She died in 1882, her life and happiness destroyed by an assassin's bullet and a parade of con artists.

Queen Victoria and Prince Albert were reportedly involved in spiritualism starting in 1846. In 1861, Prince Albert succumbed to what was diagnosed as typhoid fever. (There is some modern debate over the actual cause of his death.) Later, a thirteen-year-old boy, Robert James Lees, conducted a séance in which the deceased prince spoke to Victoria using a pet name known only to the couple. The teenage medium later conducted séances in Windsor Castle.[168]

As the practice spread across the United States, Ohio became a hotbed for spiritualism. One of the most famous mediums in the 1800s was Jonathan Koons of Athens, Ohio. In 1852, Koons, an avowed atheist, attended a séance with the purpose of exposing the fraudulent activities of a young lady medium, Mary Jane Paston. However, the medium informed him that he was a natural medium, and the spirits wanted to recruit him.

He was already unknowingly connected to the mystical, as his family farm was located in the Mount Nebo region of Athens, an area considered spiritually powerful by the Shawnees. Koons and his wife, Florence, soon became popular mediums, supposedly guided by the spirit of the famed pirate Henry Morgan. Together, they contacted what they called pre-

Left: It was Mary Todd Lincoln, not her husband, who was the true believer in spiritualism. She was victimized by numerous mediums. *Library of Congress.*

Right: After the death of Prince Albert, Queen Victoria of Britain permitted a thirteen-year-old boy to conduct séances in Windsor Castle. *Library of Congress.*

Adamic souls—those who were older than the six thousand years that the earth had existed before biblical creation. These primeval souls were under the guidance of an angel named Oress.

These pre-Adamic souls, along with their angelic guide, directed Koons to turn a storage building into a séance room, including assembling a bizarre contraption with moving parts that made strange noises. There were also instruments played by invisible hands and the sound of a beautiful choir. Henry Morgan or another spirit guide named King would speak through a trumpet.

It was not easy to travel to Mount Nebo, but hundreds of people made the long journey so they could experience contact with the spirit world and their departed loved ones.[169]

As spiritualism grew in popularity, there were a number of reporters and investigators who were engaged in attempting to expose them. One of these was in the 1860s in Sandusky County. Almon Bruce French, often known as A.B., was engaged as a medium for a closet séance in the home of another medium, Elsie Crindle. A sharp-eyed observer was peeking in through the window, studying what A.B. was up to. He came to the conclusion that the phenomenon was accomplished by the medium wearing masks.

He was absolutely right. The authorities investigated, found the masks, several dresses to be worn by Mrs. Crindle, some rubber tubing and, as is used often today, a great deal of gauze. Soon, the Crindles had to reach into their pocket to pay a hefty five-dollar fine.[170]

In September 1867, Cleveland hosted the fourth annual National Convention of Spiritualists. On the third day, they tackled the problem of correcting some bad press resulting from a statement made at the third annual National Convention of Spiritualists: "Before we, as Spiritualists, will consent to have the infallibility of the Bible, the deity of Jesus, and the political authority of these quondam friends of God crammed down on our souls as part of the Constitution of our Republic, we will fight till the buzzards are gorged with the spoils."[171] For some reason, they thought that this might possibly be considered offensive. They renounced it as not reflecting their beliefs and then went on to speak out in favor of Natives Americans.

One of the most popular methods used by spiritualists in the Gilded Age was the practice of spirit photography. This purports to be taking a regular photograph with the assistance of a medium, and on being developed, it will have the recognizable image of a dead person miraculously appearing in the completed picture. In those times, the science behind the new technology of photography was not known by the average person. Since those early days, most of these photographs have been debunked as outright frauds—usually the result of double exposure with the ghostly image put in during the developing process.

However, not all such examples are so easily dismissed. What if the spectral image is not simply a random dweller from beyond the veil but rather a person known to the viewer but not to the medium? Such was the case of a man in 1905, who was working on a job in Warren County.

The man had to be at his assignment throughout the winter, so he decided that it would be best to bring his family with him. During their stay, the people encountered a couple who were devout—indeed fanatical—spiritualists. The couple did their best to convert the man and his wife, but regardless, they were not in the least bit interested in dealing with ghosts. However, after a great deal of urging, they were at last able to induce them to sit for a session of spirit photography. Thinking it was all nonsense but still wanting a nice picture, they consented. However, when the photograph was developed, they were in for quite a shock.

Supposedly through the efforts of the medium, the photograph clearly showed the image of the wife's sister sitting next to her. The curious thing is, the sister had been dead for an entire decade. The husband was not left out, as next to him was the unmistakable image of his father, just as he had appeared in the very last years before he passed away.

The couple was amazed but not enough to join in with the rather evangelical conjurers. As they could find no rational explanation for this, they simply concluded, "The whole world is a mystery."[172]

It was revealed in a Cincinnati trial of a medium that what was known as a Blue Book circulated among mediums, which contained "names and intimate personal facts about prominent patrons of Spiritualism. It also contained names and descriptions of departed relatives of these persons."[173]

On December 4, 1926, Cincinnati received a visit from the person who may be considered to be the rock star of mediums, the infamous Margery. Her actual name was Mina Goddard, and she and her husband, noted surgeon Dr. Le Roi Goddard Crandon of Boston, were treated like royalty by members of the Cincinnati Psychical Society. They were the invited guests of Dr. Eric R. Twatchman. After the lecture at Memorial Hall, the two were the guests of honor at an extravagant banquet at the Sinton Hotel on Fourth Street.

Margery, the pseudonym of Mrs. Crandon, gained worldwide fame in the early 1920s, when the prestigious magazine *Scientific American* decided to run a contest on mediums. It offered a generous cash prize for anyone who could demonstrate to a jury that they had the power to create actual miracles in the séance room and perform verifiable communication with the dead.

A few mediums did submit to the rigorous exams, and one by one, they were exposed as frauds. Most of the professional clairvoyants were savvy enough to steer clear of such a test, realizing that their trickery would be revealed.

These were happy times for spiritualists. All of this occurred only a few years after World War I, when so many families had lost young men, followed by the horrific influenza pandemic, which took even more victims. Distraught family members were paying good money to mediums to make a final contact with their loved ones. The cause of spiritualism was being championed by the noted physicist Sir Oliver Lodge. Even more illustrious, and more publicly, was the wholehearted support given by the famed author Sir Arthur Conan Doyle, creator of Sherlock Holmes.

Into this mix came the well-publicized contest. The *Scientific America* team even went as far as Berlin and ended up exposing Germany's leading medium as a complete fraud. However, Margery was different. She was young, attractive, worldly and, above all, extremely charismatic. The wife of

Early spirit photographs were products of double exposures, but as the technology was new, many people did not know that the pictures were fakes. *Library of Congress.*

Arthur Conan Doyle, creator of Sherlock Holmes, was an ardent supporter of spiritualism. He wrote a book about the existence of fairies. *Library of Congress.*

a wealthy surgeon and a member in good standing of the upper crust of Boston, there was no financial motive for her to engage in trickery. Gathering with members of what was called the ABC Club, she was able to create amazing phenomena using the power of her deceased brother, Walter.

Some critics stated that she was more than just the proper upper-class hostess; she was out and out flirtatious. There were ugly rumors that she was even trying to seduce members of the examination team.

At first, no one could find any trickery. However, the final member of the jury saw her and knew immediately that she was a complete fraud. He was the master magician and escape artist Harry Houdini. Houdini claimed that Margery had attempted to seduce him. He found an extendable tape measure concealed in the séance closet (mediums were often put into such devices, supposedly to prevent trickery by touching items), a device that could be used to extend her reach out of the box to manipulate trumpets and other devices in the room.

He devised an apparatus that would prevent her from having any use of her hands or legs during the séance. While some complained that it was like a medieval pillory, Margery agreed to the test. She should not have. Restrained from using her limbs, there was no phenomenon. Needless to say, the prize was not awarded.

Later, a group of Harvard scientists attempted to test her. She thought that without the prying eyes of a stage magician this would be easy; however, the scientists were more on-the-ball than she expected. They discovered that she was something of a contortionist and was able to manipulate objects and even touch the sitters in the dark room with her feet. With that exposure, even without the assistance of Houdini, her reputation as a valid medium was now relegated only to the truest of believers. One might say that she "tranced" to the choir.

In her 1926 Cincinnati visit, she was questioned about Harry Houdini, who had died unexpectedly a little over a month before her visit to the Queen City. Margery was asked if he had tried to contact her. She said no, but he

Harry Houdini was the spiritualists' greatest foe. While supposed experts could be fooled by mediums like Margery, Houdini always exposed their trickery. *Library of Congress.*

was probably a bit confused by his new surroundings. She also proceeded to lie about the earlier tests and mock those who had tried to examine her claims to supernatural power.

Margery remains a mystery, as she had no monetary gain to attain from the séances and had a reputation to lose.[174]

One of the most famous séances held in Ohio was at the Palace Theater in Columbus in the 1970s. A medium invited the noted stage magician Harry Blackstone Jr. and some of his companions to join in the procedure. The object was to contact the spirit of Thurston the Magician.

One member of Blackstone's group did not participate but simply watched from the sidelines. The medium was possessed by a man who had supposedly died in the building. When the séance was over, the medium angrily turned around and demanded to know why the bystander did not participate. She ordered him to go into a balcony area of the theater and see what was up there waiting for him.

As skeptical as he was, the man nonetheless did as she asked. But when he reached the balcony, a strange, invisible force came over him, nearly crushing the life out of him. Catching his breath and leaving much faster than he had arrived, he returned to the group. He tried to dismiss the inexplicable feeling that he had up there.

Everyone in the group, save for the medium, was standing with their mouths open. While he was gone, she had predicted everything that he had just said.[175]

We shall conclude our journey the same way: mouth open, eyes staring and muttering that there are some mighty strange things in the Buckeye State. There are indeed some very creepy things lurking in the furrows of cornfields, roaming through dense forests at night and prowling silently through the dark alleys of major cities.

When photographer Douglas R. Weise and I visited Cedar Hill Cemetery in Newark in Licking County to take photographs of the Baker mausoleum and the Baby Face grave, we parked on the roadway below a short hill. As we walked up the rise, our minds were on less than spiritual concerns. We were discussing where we would go for lunch, wondering if there were any good restaurants in Newark.

While walking up, Mr. Weise suddenly turned to me and asked, "Do you smell flowers?"

I did indeed. I looked around to see if there were fresh flowers, but this was an old section, and there were no such displays. But he was right—there was not just the smell of flowers, but it was as if someone had taken a bouquet of fresh roses and rubbed them in my face. The flowery scent was overpowering. But walking only about two steps farther, there was not the slightest trace of any floral aroma. It was only in that one particular spot, while walking past nineteenth-century graves. When we were finished, we walked down the same hill, but there was no flowery smell whatsoever.

In Victorian times, funerals were held in private homes. Mounds of fresh flowers were brought in and placed around coffins to mask the inevitable odor of decomposition. What did we smell? Was it just a spring breeze—or was it someone from a previous century letting us know that although their names are forgotten, they are still around?

From the coils of that enigmatic serpent in Adams County to the life-sucking cabin in the Black Swamp to the strange horseshoe on the grave in Perry County to the headless horsemen charging up the country roads in the moonlight and right down to the feather crowns growing in your mattress, there is no doubt that Ohio can be a very strange place.

Personally, I'm ready to believe the supernatural lore of Ohio. Except for the ghost cow climbing into the wagon. I'll pass on that one.

NOTES

Introduction

1. F.W Putnam, *Century Illustrated Monthly Magazine* 29 (April 1890).
2. "Serpent Mound Crater, Ohio," United States Meteorite Impact Craters, 2016, https://impactcraters.us.
3. "Serpent Mound," History, updated August 21, 2018, https://www.history.com.
4. Ibid.
5. Putnam, *Century Illustrated Monthly*.
6. Job 26:13 (King James Version).
7. "The Serpent Lesson," Ohio History Connection, Ohio History Center, February 2014, https://www.ohiohistory.org.
8. Alan Johnson, "Vandals Admit Muffin-Crystal-Thingie Assault at Serpent Mound," *Columbus Dispatch*, November 2, 2012, https://www.dispatch.com.
9. "Wilhelm Reich Austrian Psychologist," Encyclopedia Britannica, March 20, 2019, https://www.britannica.com.
10. David Weatherly, "Serpent Mound UFO Sighting," *Two Crows Paranormal* (blog), January 11, 2017, http://twocrowsparanormal.blogspot.com.
11. Paul Devereux, *Places of Power: Secret Energies at Ancient Sites: A Guide to Observed or Measured Phenomena* (London: Blandford, 1990), 191–2.
12. "The Great Serpent Mound," Great Serpent Mound of Southern Ohio, http://www.greatserpentmound.com.

Chapter 1

13. Montague Summers, *The Vampire: His Kith and Kin* (New York: University Books, 1960), 142.

14. Faire, "Sarah Tillinghast," *Fairweather Lewis* (blog), April 27, 2010, https://fairweatherlewis.wordpress.com.

15. Doug MacGowan, "The Mercy Brown Vampire Story," Historic Mysteries, October 14, 2016, https://www.historicmysteries.com.

16. Moncure Daniel Conway, *Demonology and Devil-Lore* (New York: Henry Holt, 1897), 51.

17. Eugene B. Willard, *A Standard History of the Hanging Rock Iron Region of Ohio: An Authentic Narrative of the Past, with an Extended Survey of the Industrial and Commercial Development*, vol. 1 (N.p.: Lewis Publishing, 1916), 43–44.

18. Henry Howe, *Historical Collections of Ohio in Two Volumes* (Cincinnati, OH: C.J. Krehbiel & Co., 1907), 568.

19. Summers, *Vampire*, 18.

20. *Cincinnati Enquirer*, January 8, 1885.

21. *Piqua Daily Call*, January 21, 1897.

22. *Cincinnati Enquirer*, March 22, 1879.

23. Ibid., January 31, 1892.

24. *Cincinnati Enquirer*, September 28, 1889, 4.

25. Chris Woodyard, *Haunted Ohio III: Still More Ghostly Tales from the Buckeye State* (Beavercreek, OH: Kestrel Publications, 1994), 197.

26. Mary Jones, "Bean Sidhe," Jones Celtic Encyclopedia, 2004, http://www.ancienttexts.org.

27. "Banshees and Warnings," Visions and Beliefs in the West of Ireland: Banshees and Warnings, http://www.sacred-texts.com.

28. Sandy Smith, "Haunted Dayton: Ghost Stories of the Gem City," *Dayton Most Metro*, October 27, 2010, http://www.mostmetro.com.

29. Lafcadio Hearn, *Period of the Gruesome: Selected Cincinnati Journalism of Lafcadio Hearn*, ed. Jon C. Hughes (Lanham, MD: University Press of America, 1990), 241.

30. *Cincinnati Enquirer*, May 13, 1892.

31. Ibid., May 27, 1892.

32. "Loveland's Frogman," Weird Ohio, http://www.weirdus.com.

33. Dana Matthews, "Ohio's Mysterious Loveland Castle Is Haunted by the Ghost of Its Creator," Week in Weird. January 5, 2017, http://weekinweird.com.

34. Chris Woodyard, *Haunted Ohio: Ghostly Tales from the Buckeye State* (Beavercreek, OH: Kestrel Publications, 1994), 198.

35. Chris Woodyard, *Haunted Ohio IV: Restless Spirits* (Beavercreek, OH: Kestrel Publications, 1997), 157.

36. "Mythical Creatures Guide," Dullahan—Mythical Creatures Guide, August 19, 2011, http://www.mythicalcreaturesguide.com.

37. Jannette Quackenbush, *Ohio Ghost Hunter Guide VI: Haunted Hocking* (Hocking Hills, OH: 21 Crows Dusk to Dawn Publishing, 2014), 128.

38. "Guernsey County Ohio Ghosts and Hauntings—Headless Man of Londonderry," Ohio Ghost Stories and Spooky Legends, www.hauntedhocking.com.

39. "Belmont County Hauntings & Legends," Ohio Exploration Society, September 24, 2018, www.ohioexploration.com.

40. Quackenbush, *Ohio Ghost Hunter VI*, 207.

41. Michael Kleen, "The Many Mysteries of Rogues Hollow Road," *M.A. Kleen* (blog), February 19, 2019, michaelkleen.com.

42. Quackenbush, *Ohio Ghost Hunter VI*, 229.

43. Jannette Quackenbush, *Ohio Ghost Hunter Guide V: Haunted Hocking* (Hocking Hills, OH: 21 Crows Dusk to Dawn Publishing, 2013), 130.

Chapter 2

44. *Cincinnati Gazette*, March 7, 1879.

45. "More Wonders of the Invisible World," *Ohio Memory* (blog), May 29, 2015, ohiohistoryhost.org.

46. I. Marc Carlson, Historical Witches and Witchtrials in North America, June 13, 2011, www.personal.utulsa.edu.

Chapter 3

47. Henry B. Teetor, *The Past and Present of Mill Creek Valley* (Cincinnati, OH: Cohen & Co., 1882), 49.

48. Ibid.

49. Ibid., 51.

50. Luke 11.

51. Jacob Grimm, *Teutonic Mythology*, vol. 2 (London: George Bell, 1883), 629.

52. Colonel William Monroe Cockrum, *Pioneer History of Indiana Including Stories, Incidents and Customs of the Early Settlers* (Oakland, IN: Press of Oakland City Journal, 1907), 340.
53. Ibid.
54. Ibid., 341.
55. Chris Woodyard, *The Headless Horror: Strange and Ghostly Ohio Tales* (Dayton, OH: Kestrel Publications, 2013), 109.
56. *Cist's Advertiser*, January 7, 1845.
57. Ibid.
58. J.L. Wilson, *A Sermon on Witchcraft* (Cincinnati, OH: First Presbyterian Church, November 9, 1845).
59. Ibid.
60. Ibid.
61. Ibid.
62. Ibid.
63. *Cincinnati Enquirer*, August 19, 1964.
64. *Washington Post*, January 15, 1929.

Chapter 4

65. *Cincinnati Enquirer*, April 19, 1898.
66. Ibid., March 11, 1885.
67. *Cincinnati Enquirer*, March 11, 1885.
68. Dion Fortune, *Psychic Self-Defense* (York Beach, ME: Samuel Weiser, 2001), 9.
69. *Cincinnati Commercial*, March 7, 1879.
70. Carl Sferrazza Anthony, *Florence Harding: The First Lady, the Jazz Age, and the Death of America's Most Scandalous President* (New York: W. Morrow, 1999), 175.
71. Quackenbush, *Ohio Ghost Hunter VI*, 217.
72. "Is Anna Mary Stockum a Witch Searching for Her Head?" Ok, Ok, February 4, 2018, newcomerstown.com.
73. "Fairfield County Hauntings & Legends," Ohio Exploration Society, November 9, 2017, www.ohioexploration.com.

Chapter 5

74. Frederick Thomas Elworthy, *The Evil Eye: An Account of This Ancient and Widespread Superstition* (London: John Murray, 1895), 3.
75. Woodyard, *Headless Horror*, 116.

76. Tammy Rose, "Death Crowns: A Creepy Piece of Appalachia's Folklore," *Got Mountain Life*, September 25, 2018, gotmountainlife.com.

77. *Cincinnati Enquirer*, September 12, 1875.

78. Ibid.

79. Ibid., May 29, 1881.

80. Ibid.

81. Ibid.

82. Ibid., March 27, 1883.

83. *Cincinnati Commercial Gazette*, March 27, 1883.

84. Ibid.

85. Ibid.

86. Ibid., March 28, 1883.

Chapter 6

87. "The Lincoln Funeral Train," Ghosts of Ohio, Lore & Legends, www.ghostsofohio.org.

88. Woodyard, *Haunted Ohio IV*, 10.

89. "Jackson County Ohio Ghosts and Hauntings—Lake Alma State Park," Ohio Ghost Stories and Spooky Legends, www.hauntedhocking.com.

90. "Paranormal Activity," Merry Go Round Museum, 2013, www.merrygoroundmuseum.org.

91. Al Hunter, "The Ghosts of Kings Island, Part 1," *Weekly View*, May 16, 2013, weeklyview.net.

92. *Cincinnati Enquirer*, December 28, 1896.

93. Woodyard, *Haunted Ohio III*, 136.

94. Quackenbush, *Ohio Ghost Hunter VI*, 152.

95. Jannette Quackenbush and Patrick Quackenbush, *Haunted Hocking: A Ghost Hunters Guide to the Hocking Hills...and Beyond II* (self-published, CreateSpace, 2011), 125.

96. "Legends & Mysteries," DustyBlues Fine Art Photography, www.dustyblues.com.

97. "Otterbein Cemetery—Bloody Horseshoe Grave," Ghosts of Ohio, Lore & Legends, 2008, www.ghostsofohio.org.

98. "Ripley, Ohio Ghost Sightings," Ghost Sightings of America, www.ghostsofamerica.com.

99. *Cleveland Plain Dealer*, May 26, 2001.

100. Paul Carus, *The History of the Devil and the Idea of Evil from the Earliest Times to the Present Day* (Chicago: Open Court Publishing, 1900), 252–53.
101. "Top 12 Most Haunted Places in Dayton, OH," Haunted Rooms America, 2019, www.hauntedrooms.com.

Chapter 7

102. "Ashtabula Train Disaster of 1876," Ohio History Connection, Ohio History Central, www.ohiohistorycentral.org.
103. "About 'The Screaming Bridge of Maud Hughes Road,'" HauntWorld, 2019, www.hauntworld.com.
104. "Delaware County Ohio Ghosts and Hauntings—Blue Limestone Park," Haunted Hocking, www.hauntedhocking.com.
105. "County Historian Recalls Millfield Mine Disaster," *Athens News*, November 7, 2012, www.athensnews.com.
106. "Cleveland Torso Murders: The Work of the Mad Butcher," Historic Mysteries, February 1, 2019, www.historicmysteries.com.
107. "The Legend of the Hatchet Man (Audio Included)," Peak of Ohio, October 21, 2011, www.peakofohio.com.
108. Quackenbush, *Ohio Ghost Hunter III*, 178.
109. Albert Rosenberg and Cindy Armstrong, *The American Gladiators: Taft Versus Remus* (Hemet, CA: Aimwell Press, 1995).
110. Jen Ernke, "Henry County Hauntings & Legends," Ohio Exploration Society, October 2, 2016, https://www.ohioexploration.com.
111. "Henry County Hauntings & Legends," Ohio Exploration Society, October 2, 2016, www.ohioexploration.com.
112. *Cincinnati Enquirer*, April 10, 1875.
113. "Battle of Buffington Island," Ohio History Central, www.ohiohistorycentral.org.
114. "Battle of Buffington Island," Haunted Hocking, www.hauntedhocking.com.

Chapter 8

115. Quackenbush, *Ohio Ghost Hunter VI*, 24.
116. "The West State Angel," Athens County Visitors Bureau, 2014, athensohio.com.

117. Woodyard, *Haunted Ohio III*, 131.

118. "A Tale of Love and Murder in Egypt Valley," *Intelligencer*, October 30, 2016, www.theintelligencer.net

119. "Urban Legend Series: Library Park," *Dayton Unknown* (blog), February 28, 2014, daytonunknown.wordpress.com.

120. "Social Sharings," *Telegram News*, October 19, 2015, thetelegramnews. com.

121. "Top 10 Most Haunted Places in Columbus, OH (Updated 2019)," Haunted Rooms America, 2019, www.hauntedrooms.com.

122. "Goll Woods Cemetery," *Fringe Paranormal* (blog), July 12, 2011, fringeparanormal.wordpress.com.

123. "Gallia County Ohio Ghosts and Hauntings—Tyn Rhos Cemetery," Haunted Hocking, www.hauntedhocking.com.

124. "Meigs County Hauntings & Legends," Ohio Exploration Society, October 2, 2016, www.ohioexploration.com.

125. "Pickaway County Hauntings & Legends," Ohio Exploration Society, September 24, 2018, https://www.ohioexploration.com.

126. "Cholera Cemetery," Ohio History Connection, Ohio History Central, www.ohiohistorycentral.org.

127. Quackenbush, *Ohio Ghost Hunter V*, 216.

128. Karyn Locke, "Haunted History of Marietta, Ohio: 7 Spooky, Kooky, Crazy Tales," *Sand and Snow* (blog), April 12, 2017, www.sandandorsnow. com.

129. "Vinton County Hauntings & Legends," Ohio Exploration Society, October 2, 2016, www.ohioexploration.com.

130. "Hamilton County Ohio Ghosts and Hauntings," Haunted Hocking, www.hauntedhocking.com.

131. Charlotte Guest, trans., *The Mabinogion* (Woodstock, ON: Devoted Publishing, 2018), 122.

132. *Cincinnati Enquirer*, January 19, 1908.

133. "Fall 2017," *This Is Findlay Magazine*, www.thisisfindlay.com.

134. Quackenbush and Quackenbush, *Haunted Hocking*, 113.

Chapter 9

135. *Cincinnati Times Star*, November 11, 1953.

136. Chris Woodyard, *Haunted Ohio II: More Ghostly Tales from the Buckeye State* (Beavercreek, OH: Kestrel Publishing, 1992), 177.

137. "Classic Columbus Ghost Stories: The Columbus Poltergeist," *Columbus Monthly*, October 19, 2015, https://www.columbusmonthly.com.

138. Woodyard, *Haunted Ohio II*, 53.

139. "Scioto County Ohio Ghosts and Hauntings—Shawnee State University," Haunted Hocking, https://www.hauntedhocking.com.

140. "'The Kissing Ghost of Greenfield Ohio'—Highland County—Tuesday, October 26, 2010—Parade Starting at 6:00 p.m.," *Exploring Almost Forgotten Gravesites in the Great State of Ohio* (blog), October 23, 2010, https://limesstones.blogspot.com.

141. Nancy D. Brown, "The Golden Lamb: Ohio's Oldest Hotel—Historic and Haunted," *What a Trip* (blog), August 24, 2017, https://www.nancydbrown.com.

142. "A Haunting in Ohio: The 'Haunted' Hotels of the Buckeye State," Ohio Memory, October 30, 2015, https://ohiomemory.ohiohistory.org.

143. Jim Ingram, "7 Things You Probably Don't Know About This Iconic Dayton Building," Dayton, February 15, 2017, https://www.dayton.com.

144. "Montgomery County Hauntings & Legends," Ohio Exploration Society, September 24, 2018, https://www.ohioexploration.com.

145. Ross Williams, "Ghost Hunters Find Evidence of Paranormal Activity at Cool Beans Coffee Roasters," *Marietta Daily Journal*, October 19, 2018, https://www.mdjonline.com.

146. "Ohio Theatre—Columbus, OH," Waymarking, January 9, 2010, http://www.waymarking.com.

147. Woodyard, *Haunted Ohio V*, 92.

148. "Monitor School," *Theresa's Haunted History of the Tri-State* (blog), January 1, 1970, http://theresashauntedhistoryofthetri-state.blogspot.com.

149. "Spooky Places on Campus," *Ohio State Online*, January 3, 2019, https://online.osu.edu.

150. Woodyard, *Haunted Ohio IV*, 15.

151. "Haunted Attractions in Zanesville, Ohio," Miller-Valentine Residential Property Management, October 17, 2018, https://yournextplacetolive.com.

152. "The Stories Behind These 9 Haunted Bridges in Ohio Will Keep You Up at Night," Only in Your State, August 26, 2016, https://www.onlyinyourstate.com.

153. "Wayne County Ohio Ghosts and Hauntings," Rogues Hollow, Haunted Hocking, https://www.hauntedhocking.com.

154. "Legend Tripping: Exploring Lorain County Hauntings," Visit Lorain County, August 6, 2014, http://www.visitloraincounty.com.

155. "Haunted Places in Circleville, Ohio," Haunted Places, https://www.hauntedplaces.org.

156. *Cincinnati Commercial Gazette*, August 29, 1875.

157. Ibid.

Chapter 10

158. Ibid.

159. "Utopia," *Creepy Cincinnati* (blog), July 19, 2016, https://creepycincinnati.com.

160. Author private correspondence with Ron Hill, Clermont County Historical Society, 2019.

161. *Cincinnati Enquirer*, March 26, 1883.

162. Ibid.

163. Allen Spraggett, *The Psychic Mafia* (New York: St. Martin's Press, 1976).

164. Karen Abbott, "The Fox Sisters and the Rap on Spiritualism," *Smithsonian Magazine*, October 30, 2012, https://www.smithsonianmag.com.

165. *Cincinnati Enquirer*, September 14, 1856.

166. Ibid.

167. "Mary's Charlatans: Nettie Colburn (1841–1892)," Mr. Lincoln's White House, Lehrman Institute, http://www.mrlincolnswhitehouse.org.

168. "Medium Rare," Leicester Local History, BBC, November 13, 2014, http://www.bbc.co.uk.

169. Hatfield, Sharon. *Enchanted Ground: The Spirit Room of Jonathan Koons* (Athens, OH: Swallow Press, 2018), 55.

170. Travis Sanders, "Spiritualism in North Central Ohio," *My Truth* (blog), January 26, 2017, https://travispsychic.wordpress.com.

171. John Buescher, 1867 Cleveland Plain Dealer, http://www.iapsop.com.

172. *Cincinnati Enquirer*, August 10, 1905.

173. *Cincinnati Post*, November 12, 1914.

174. David Jaher, *The Witch of Lime Street: Séance, Seduction, and Houdini in the Spirit World* (New York: Broadway Books, 2016).

175. Woodyard, *Haunted Ohio II*, 173.

ABOUT THE AUTHOR

Steven J. Rolfes, a lifelong Ohioan, is a freelance writer and volunteer docent at the Cincinnati History Museum. He is the author of six books on history, including *The Cincinnati Court Riot*, *Cincinnati Landmarks* and *Cincinnati Under Water: The 1937 Flood*, and is coauthor of *Cincinnati Art Deco* and *Historic Downtown Cincinnati*. For years, he hosted a radio talk show on the supernatural called *Bolgia 4*. He lives in Cincinnati with his wife and two children.